HAUNTS OF OLD LOUISVILLE

*Gilded Age Ghosts
and Haunted Mansions
in
America's Spookiest Neighborhood*

by

David Dominé

D0840513

International Standard Book Number 978-1-934898-05-5
Library of Congress Card Catalog Number 2009931483

Cover design and book layout by James Asher

Manufactured in the United States

All book order correspondence should be addressed to:

McClanahan Publishing House, Inc.
P.O. Box 100
Kuttawa, KY 42055

270-388-9388
800-544-6959
270-388-6186 FAX

www.kybooks.com

DEDICATION

For Rocky, a scrappy little schnauzer who rekindled my love for animals one day in March 2000 when he joined the family. I hope he catches a squirrel one of these days.

I think a Person who is thus terrified with the Imagination of Ghosts and Spectres much more reasonable, than one who contrary to the Reports of all Historians sacred and profane, ancient and modern, and to the Traditions of all Nations, thinks the Appearance of Spirits fabulous and groundless.

– Joseph Addison,
The Spectator, 1711

TABLE OF CONTENTS

PREFACE

Albert Einstein once said, "The most beautiful thing we can experience is the Mysterious," and despite his skepticism of a personal god, he apparently marveled at a higher power. People – it would seem – take joy in the supposition that something beyond our control can transcend human understanding and pierce the ethereal borders of a world where soul and spirit survive the corporeal realm. Some call these lingering shades of a former existence "ghosts" or "specters," and many connect their appearances to past tragedy, injustice, sorrow, pain and heartbreak. Others see them as comforting presences inextricably bound to a physical location.

Whatever the name or purported source of these wraithlike creatures, ghosts – without a doubt – occupy a hallowed spot at the top of the roster of paranormal occurrences. And, of all those arcane phenomena attributed to the supernatural, spectral beings have become an integral part of modern society and folklore.

What are ghosts?

I don't know exactly.

Do I believe in ghosts?

I haven't decided yet, especially given that I have never seen one. However, that doesn't mean that I doubt other people have seen or experienced things they call ghosts.

Do I believe human beings experience strange phenomena that cannot be explained away by science and coincidence?

Most assuredly. I have experienced activities myself that – apart from sheer imagination or happenstance – could only be attributed to something beyond ordinary human understanding. Even if I allow rational thought to chip away at the potential paranormal when hours of unexplained footsteps and hair-raising goings-on have caused me to flee my own house, I still relish the notion that circumstances out of my control – whatever they be – have jolted me from the mundane complacency of a workaday world and planted the seed of doubt in my mind.

About uncertainty, the great German writer Johann Wolfgang von Goethe once said, "We know accurately only when we know little, with knowledge doubt increases." William Shakespeare presaged this sentiment when he declared, "Modest doubt is called the beacon of the wise." Although I don't purport to be more knowledgeable than the average person, I – like many – have come to the firm conviction that the more you learn, the more you realize there are so many things you don't know.

Doubt, it would seem, figures prominently in the learning process, so why do so many equate doubt with weakness? Why do individuals who entertain the notion that specters may actually exist often receive the label "eccentric"? Why do so many would-be Christian scholars pooh-pooh the existence of specters or earth-bound spirits, even though the Bible makes clear mention of these things? Why do scientists often claim that science allows no room for souls and the afterlife? To my mind, only arrogance and lack of faith in one's own convictions could lead so-called rational beings to discount all phenomena outside their belief systems. And only the shortsighted would have the temerity to lay claim to total understanding of the universe in which we live.

That having been said, I see our world as a complex, marvelous place that hasn't given up all its secrets yet, and because of that, I unapologetically reserve a special space in the back of my mind for the existence of ghosts.

And if any neighborhood I know is going to harbor specters, Old Louisville stands at the top of the list. With its hundreds of grand mansions and comfortable homes where generations have lived, loved and died, it offers up a veritable smorgasbord for aficionados of wonderful architecture and local legend. It's not surprising, then, that many of these century-old dwellings come with an assortment of resident haunts and soulful phantoms in search of a bit of nostalgia.

In my previous books, I have clearly stated that I consider myself a skeptic. More often than not, people imagine explanations they would attribute to the supernatural, and I've also discovered that individuals at times fib about would-be paranormal occurrences and have fabricated circumstances that would lend credence to supposed cases of hauntings and spectral disturbances. Such is the desire to "prove" the existence of ghosts and the world of the unseen. I also realize that well-intentioned people often cross over into the realm of the overzealous and that others are sometimes just plain mistaken. But, when dealing with reported cases of the paranormal, there seems to always be a noticeable percentage – say 5 or 10 percent – of these accounts that defies rational explanation. It is this small fraction of supposed otherworldly encounters that piques my curiosity and leads me to investigate the stories that I include in my books.

Not that I want to convince anyone of anything (as I've said before, I put these stories out there for entertainment purposes and nothing more). I just want to present a story that defies explanation, or at least makes you pull the covers tighter around you at night. You can take it or leave it. Don't ask me to justify my accounts of hauntings in this book, and don't tell me that you don't believe in the supernatural, because – truth be told – I don't care.

This book comprises a collection of stories, a loosely organized record of what I have heard from (in my opinion) reputable sources with paranormal experiences that somehow tie into the historical fabric of the area. Because I rely so heavily on the spoken word for much of my information, there is an undeniably folkloric element to these tales. When I hear a story that I deem interesting, I start to research the history behind it. If I come up with a bit of fascinating historical documentation to back up the story, all the better – it merits inclusion in my books. This is not meant to be a scholarly work, but rather an entertaining collection of tales that weaves together eyewitness accounts and local history.

I've also stated before that I am not a historian or a parapsychologist. Because of that, this book is offered neither as a historical work nor as a study of the paranormal. Another thing I am not is a ghost hunter. Yes, I do hunt down ghost stories, but that's as far as it goes. Although I occasionally tag along on psychic investigations with various paranormal investigative teams, I do so as a mere observer, and I profess to have none of the scientific expertise (or patience) that would enable me to conduct an authentic psychic investigation. As I've said before, I'm just a curious individual with a penchant for supposedly haunted places who collects information and then writes it down in story form. That's it.

The tales in this book add to a rich collection of folklore and legend that sheds light on paranormal events and purportedly haunted places in Old Louisville. As with my other books, some of these stories appear as first-hand accounts of unearthly happenings, while others come as legends that have taken root in the area. And, as with my previous works, one or two may have been documented before, even though most make their first appearance in this tome. In any case, each chapter in this book – as with my other books – is a story that I have crafted using historical background, recorded eyewitness accounts, facts and a modest amount of creativity. Although I make no claims as to the veracity of the information herein and offer the stories for enjoyment only, I have conducted numerous hours of research and interviewed scores of people, so there is indeed a basis in fact for many of these tales. As for the many people I interviewed, some of their names have been changed to provide anonymity. Many fear ridicule and derision, even though they do not waver in insisting that their accounts are factual. When I quote an individual and mention the name, this indicates a first-hand source I interviewed. When I quote other individuals but do not give a name, the information is second-hand. Since people often use slang or less-than-perfect grammar when reciting their accounts or writing them down for me, I have also taken the liberty of paraphrasing and editing their quotes when necessary – always subject to their final approval.

Old Louisville has a wealth of untold stories and intriguing tales, and I have truly enjoyed tracking them down. It is a marvelous place that requires only a bit of open-mindedness and a spirit of adventure to uncover charms both of this world and the next. Because of this, and my abiding fascination with all things Kentucky, my ghost stories include more than just scary details and uncanny occurrences. If I can whet your appetite with a bit of tantalizing architectural detail or the menu from a recent dinner party featuring Bluegrass cuisine, I'll do it. If a quirky character or unnecessary historical tidbit adds some color to the story, I'll include that, too. As long as it contributes to the overall feeling that Old Louisville is a unique place that deserves further exploration, it counts as fair game for me. I hope I continue to pique the curiosity of locals and outsiders alike and entice them to come and investigate the Gilded Age ghosts and haunted mansions in America's grandest Victorian neighborhood.

David Dominé
Louisville, October 31, 2008

FOREWORD

Early humans no doubt crouched around their campfires listening to a storyteller – perhaps even the group's shaman or healer – relate accounts of the specters that animated their untamed world.

They might have heard tales of the mythical spirits that were said to inhabit sacred places as a way of relating lessons about local geography and the cultural importance of such places.

Or they might have heard stories of the great deeds performed by ancestors, ghosts of a bygone era, who continued to inhabit a netherworld as protector spirits. The latter would have been stories of real people whose lives had passed into legend, narratives that preserved the band's history through retelling from generation to generation.

This ancient oral tradition, no doubt as old as language itself, continues in the fine practice of writers such as David Dominé, who collects here more than a dozen tales of earth-bound specters who still haunt Louisville's elegant Gilded Age mansions – and our imagination.

Dominé is concerned less with telling ghost stories than with recounting the history and legends of the nation's best-preserved Victorian neighborhood as seen through the ghosts who refuse to move on, away or beyond its boundaries.

His fabulous fables are as much about the people and architecture of this "lost" world as they are about the poltergeists and paranormal phenomenon modern visitors have encountered. His purpose is to inform us about local history and folklore as much as it is to frighten.

My assignments as a travel writer have taken me to Kentucky on several occasions, and I first met David on one of his justifiably well-regarded tours of the Old Louisville neighborhood he called home for so long. On a sunny day, the streets felt safe and calm until David mag-

nificently transported us back in time by conjuring the spectral beings –
practically calling up the winds that swept past us as if the spirits really
were all around us despite the midday sunshine.

I was immediately captivated, as you the reader will be, by the
stories of Sally, a phantom of unknown origin who occasionally tosses
books off the shelves at the sumptuous Ferguson Mansion (now The
Filson Historical Society), by the spectral stable hand at the carriage
house at 1366 South Third Street (now the Campion House), by the
winged demon-like apparition (could it really be Spring Heeled Jack?)
at the Walnut Street Baptist Church, or by any of the other supernatural stirrings – or are they hallucinations of over-active imaginations? –
encountered in the luxurious homes and businesses along Louisville's
Millionaires Row.

My recommendation for the ideal reading environment for
these tales: Book into one of the bed-and-breakfasts that now occupy
some of the handsome homes of the city's long-dead movers and shakers. On a cold October night, tuck yourself into bed with a hot bever-
age – or a bracing alcoholic one – to steady your nerves. (Warning:
Those faint of heart should consider reading the book in broad daylight
in a public place surrounded by friends and family.)

Was that the rustling of a satin gown in the stairwell, the laughter of young boys playing on the landing, or the crunch of an old lady's
rocking chair you heard from the front porch? Did an earth-bound spirit just cause your candle to flicker and sputter? Who left a cryptic message for you in a spidery feminine hand on the open notepad on your
desk? Read on – and spook yourself silly whenever you hear the stairs
creak or the rain whip itself against the wavy-glass windows.

This book is proof that you don't have to believe in ghosts to
cherish a great ghost story – or the goose bumps it engenders. On a
"dark and stormy night" alone in a drafty house, even the biggest skeptic is likely to become a believer with David Dominé as the spine-tin-
gling guide.

Barbara E. Cohen
Indianapolis, October 31, 2008

INTRODUCTION

A snappish afternoon in autumn, when showers of golden chestnut leaves cascade to the ground and blanket the walkways, is an ideal time to stroll the streets and alleyways of America's grandest Victorian neighborhood. Although the entire district holds many charms in store, one street in particular has special allure for lovers of the Gilded Age, that period of unprecedented economic and industrial growth during the latter half of the 19th century in America that led to an explosion of wealth in the middle and upper classes. For the higher echelons, it was a time of unbridled opulence that culminated in lavish parties and near-decadent displays of prosperity – until the advent of income taxes and the brewing storm clouds of the Panic of 1893 brought the extravagant era to an end.

Although the excessive grandeur that so typified that Gilded Age has long since faded, physical specimens of the grand era still remain scattered throughout the country in the form of impressive residences in larger cities and upscale resort communities. The Bluegrass State saw its share of Gilded Age homes, and many of them still dot the Old Louisville Historic Preservation District, where Third Street – originally known as Third Avenue – would emerge as a bastion for the elite of the city. A large portion of these stately homes came as a direct result of an unprecedented boom in local construction spurred by the world-famous Southern Exposition, which drew hundreds of thousands of visitors to its ornate exhibit hall between 1883 and 1887. In 1885 alone, some 280 mansions went up near Third Avenue, and entrepreneurial architects and designers could barely keep up with the demand for impressive abodes with state-of-the-art amenities and aesthetic furnishings. Bankers and merchants took up residence in palatial dwellings, and tobacco barons constructed comfortable, opulent homes next to wealthy distillers and the movers and shakers associated with the burgeoning thoroughbred industry.

Samuel Culbertson, son of Indiana's wealthiest man and one of the first presidents of nearby Churchill Downs, built an opulent 52-room mansion in the 1400 block in 1897, and in that same year wholesale shoe magnate William Thalheimer took up residence in a magnificent chateauesque residence across the street. Their Third Street neighbors included the talented Ainslie family, whose patriarch had gained some renown as a poet in his native Scotland, and the Fergusons, whose opulent Beaux Arts mansion cost an unheard-of $100,000 when completed in 1905. Other residents of note included the Grabfelders, Bernheims, Campions, Speeds, Middletons and the Gathrights, and their comfortable homes became some of the most envied in all of Louisville.

These lavish dwellings saw more than a century of history replete with family drama, financial woes, celebration and sorrow, and all of these events would leave their mark on the splendid homes along Third Street. Today, their stories linger on in the neighborhood, and many residents regale visitors to these storied mansions with tales of unexplained footsteps, cold chills, forlorn wails and sad moans. Whether or not all of these stories have a basis in fact has yet to be seen. However, local lore has imbued these palatial homes with a multitude of ghostly denizens and otherworldly haints, and legend has given rise to characters as real as any of the modern-day inhabitants of Old Louisville. These shades of a former existence live on in the hearts and minds of countless Old Louisvillians, and whether you believe in them or not, they are here to stay.

Although October is their preferred month, the specters of Old Louisville frequent the streets of America's grandest Victorian neighborhood all year long, and their favorite haunts naturally include the splendid Gilded Age mansions that still survive in Old Louisville. Softly trodding a cold hallway after dark, peeking out from behind an ornately carved bedpost washed in the light of a full moon, or quietly hiding at the back of a dusty closet while gray clouds gather overhead and rumble and shake with thunder, the specters of Old Louisville have made themselves at home in the opulent mansions in this, America's largest Victorian neighborhood. They lurk in the shadows and wait for a kindred soul in the living before they allow a fleeting glimpse of the world beyond, a plain populated with feathery apparitions, lost souls and confused spirits. But before the sun has risen, they have receded into the faded damask and baize within the elegant interiors of the Gilded Age homes that dot Old Louisville, and there they wait for the next sunset before their shadows venture forth and steal through the night. Although they sometimes lurk in the cold, black air around the old gas lamps in the neighborhood, these ghosts of a bygone era are creatures of comfort by nature, and they prefer the warm parlors of these graceful homes where memory and nostalgia still linger. Doleful and tragic, the specters of Old Louisville sit and wait for you, begging your attention, in search of a kindly ear.

EVEN MORE ABOUT OLD LOUISVILLE

Little by little, Old Louisville has emerged as a wonderful example of a historic preservation in a country sadly disassociated from its past. Whereas other cities around the nation have seen many of their historic structures flattened in the name of progress and replaced by ugly parking lots and shoddy construction, Louisville has managed to save a good deal – although unfortunately only a small fraction – of the original architecture that at one time graced the city. Possessed of a disposable society where even its buildings are thrown away with shortsighted abandon, the United States has always been a country obsessed with tearing down the old and putting up the new.

Nonetheless, the historically minded are slowly gaining ground in this country, and today old homes and aged structures are en vogue, although many historic preservationists are still looked upon as somewhat eccentric, and maybe a bit threatening. Old Louisville – an area blessed with its fair share of these old homes – has been said to be the third largest historic preservation district in the nation, a wonderfully preserved time capsule and vibrant neighborhood that offers just a sample of the beautiful architecture and styles of urban living that at one time defined city life across the United States. This diamond in the rough counts as the first historic preservation district in the nation to bill itself as "America's Largest Victorian Neighborhood," and this recognition engenders fierce pride in the locals. Although several other historic neighborhoods may be larger in both area and the number of structures contained therein, no other district can claim such a high concentration of almost exclusively Victorian construction in such a contained area.

In the roughly fifty square blocks that comprise modern-day Old Louisville, some 90 percent of the storied old mansions and town homes emerged at the height of the Victorian era, which spanned roughly from 1837 to 1901. Today, they constitute one of the most brilliant collections of antique houses in the country. "The boundaries of Old Louisville frame an architectural mosaic of tremendous stylistic variety and incredible visual richness which constitutes one of the most outstanding collections of Victorian domestic architecture in America," wrote historian William Morgan in his essay "A Legacy in Architecture."

In a neighborhood renowned for its impressive architecture, Third Street has been recognized as one of the most significant stretches of antique residential architecture in the entire nation. In addition, craftsmen and artisan builders from this very region constructed most of these houses from locally quarried stone and hand-pressed brick, a characteristic that adds to the uniqueness of the structures. This high concentration of brick and stone construction serves as a good indicator of the city's wealth back in the day when these materials counted as the most costly in the architect's budget. It also ensured a lasting existence for those creations fortunate enough to evade the fury of the wrecking ball.

Paranormal experts suggest that these solid foundations and thick walls might account for the high level of supernatural activity in the area, given that the firm construction retains energy that may create a threshold to a misunderstood dimension. The Gilded Age mansions in Old Louisville have been home to generations of families that have experienced heartbreak, joy, sorrow and tragedy, and it's not surprising that some of these feelings would inevitably linger on.

An unhurried walk along the tree-shaded streets of Old Louisville transports the modern visitor back to this period more than a hundred years ago when people took an inordinate amount of pride in home, hearth and the domestic arts. The boulevards, avenues and bricked alleys of America's largest Victorian neighborhood are lined with hundreds of grand homes and elegant mansions sporting an assortment of architectural styles from all corners of the globe. Dramatic examples of Chateauesque, Richardsonian Romanesque, Italianate, Victorian

Gothic, Beaux Arts, Craftsman, Queen Anne and Georgian Revival homes stand next to more modest shotgun structures and simple frame houses. These residences share space with eclectic conglomerations of Victorian Vernacular, Arts and Crafts, Renaissance Revival, Art Nouveau and Tudor-style homes as well. Residents of Old Louisville drew upon locally grown architectural talent, much of it unbound to contemporary trends in Europe and on the East Coast of the U.S. Because of this, early builders in Old Louisville borrowed and mixed styles, imbuing the neighborhood with an exuberance of architectural techniques that at times defies categorization.

One thing remains true, however: The vibrant residences that grace the streets of Old Louisville count as more than just specimens of architecture or mansions with a colorful past. They serve as visible mementos of a long-gone era that assemble and store images that have imprinted themselves indelibly on the fabric of past domesticity. Not only that, they have become havens for spectral shadows and denizens of the netherworld. These are the chance spirits and phantoms that prefer to loiter in the shadows and around the corner rather than creep forth into the daylight and make themselves known.

Thousands of people have discovered that Old Louisville offers an unbelievable visual banquet for lovers of history and architecture. Its impressive mansions of the Gilded Age make it one of the most splendid residential districts in the entire country, one with a very haunted past indeed. Many claim that it might even be the most haunted neighborhood in the U.S.

For information about tours of haunted Old Louisville, call the Visitors Center in Historic Old Louisville at (502) 637-2922 or go online at www.ghostsofoldlouisville.com. The haunts of Old Louisville and their Gilded Age mansions are waiting for you.

Haunted Old Louisville

Chapter 1

THE FERGUSON MANSION

ven before the elegant mansions of Old Louisville started springing up in what was known as the city's Southern Extension, this gritty river town had its fair share of haunts. An article in *The New York Times* of April 21, 1871, gave a brief, one-line description about Louisville's most recent spectral sighting when it reported that "(a) headless ghost perambulates Louisville o' nights." A popular lithograph of the day illustrated a ghostly encounter at one of the city's famed brothels in which call girls – mysteriously manipulated by unseen hands – tumbled through the air with levitating champagne bottles and pieces of furniture. The caption below read: "What were they? A party of alleged spooks raised old Cain and smashed the furniture in the bagnio of Annie Jones, Louisville, Kentucky." A July 10 piece in the *Louisville Journal* of 1866 thrilled readers by writing a "ghost, whose nocturnal peregrinations on the neighborhood of the bridge over Silver Creak [sic] have caused some considerable excitement, still insists on chasing people."

So, when one of the grandest – if not the grandest – of all Old Louisville homes went up on the site at 1310 South Third Street just as America's Gilded Age was drawing to a close, residents had considered the wilderness metropolis a haunted town for decades. Today this graceful structure sits, silent and hulking, as the modern world – mostly

Completed at a cost of $100,000 in 1905, the lavish Ferguson Mansion embodies the best of Beaux-Arts architecture. Today it houses The Filson Historical Society and a mischievous poltergeist by the name of Sally.

oblivious to the stories and splendor within – passes it by. Imposing in scale, the soaring blend of beautiful details such as intricate carving, quoining, and large windows softened by Art Nouveau curves nonetheless present a visage that is both regal and elegant. Protected by elaborate roof trim and numerous balustrades, the interior reflects the opulence of another time. It is also rumored that a specter or two might lurk behind its solid walls.

Known as the Ferguson Mansion, the massive structure features elements of the Beaux Arts style, a fashion that culminated in popularity in the waning days of the 19th century. The Beaux Arts approach to architecture originated with the principles of the famous school of design by the same name in Paris, and a number of elements, particularly those focusing on extraordinary detail and symmetry, characterize the style. As with the Ferguson Mansion, Beaux Arts buildings often excel in proportion and design, and this residence typifies many features of the Beaux Arts style, such as exterior surfaces with ornamental garlands and swags, intricate floral patterns and shields. An oval cartouche adorns the main entryway, and a porch roof supported by classical columns and a mansard roof garnished with stone balustrade round out the view from the street. Architectural historian William Morgan claims the residence "with its strict symmetry and classicist-Baroque detailing is not dissimilar to Parisian houses of the period – its grandeur more suited to the pretentions of America's Gilded Age robber barons than to Louisville's management class."

According to neighborhood records, Edwin Hite Ferguson –a member of the local management class – commissioned the Louisville architectural firm of Cobb and Dodd – the same duo responsible for designing the Seelbach Hotel and the new state capitol building in Frankfort – to design the home in 1901. Construction on the mansion wrapped up in 1905 after $100,000 had been spent, making it ten times more expensive than the average residence in the neighborhood. It was, by all accounts, by far the most expensive home in Louisville. Modern architects have suggested that a mansion of that size would cost an estimated $2 million today. Most agree, however, that the level of craftsmanship and the intricate details found throughout the home could never be replicated for that cost.

The stately mansion originally housed nine occupants, six of them servants for the three members of the Ferguson family: Edwin Hite Ferguson, his wife, Sophie Fullerton Ferguson, and their daughter, Margaret. Mr. Ferguson amassed his fortune in the cottonseed-oil business, and his company grew to be the second largest such enterprise in the world. In 1907, not long after workers put the finishing touches on the mansion, his own company ousted him, and from that point on Ferguson's fortune began to dwindle, eventually forcing the sale of the house in 1924. The Pearsons, friends of the Fergusons, subsequently purchased the mansion and operated the family business there until the 1970s, when they moved to a more modern setting. In 1986, just in time for its centennial celebration, the residence became the headquarters of The Filson Historical Society.

Stepping through the front doors of Old Louisville's Ferguson Mansion plunges observers back into the past, to a time characterized by elegance, order and attention to detail. After stepping over the threshold from the ornate mosaic inlay of the front portal, they pass through heavy doors into a stately entry hall with gleaming tiles and more iridescent mosaic around the imbedded art-glass wall sconces. Up several marble steps, the hall opens onto a spacious and extravagant lobby where Mr. Ferguson often welcomed visitors and out-of-town guests. Oak paneling and ceiling coffers with a unique grain effect – achieved by the costly procedure of quarter sawing – imbue the room with a warm feeling that plays nicely against the polished hardwood flooring. An elaborately carved octagon table, constructed to match the original décor, remains in the eye-catching room where various social affairs such as Margaret Ferguson's debutante party occurred.

One newspaper society column reported that the mansion "was ablaze with lights as it was being readied for the coming out party of Miss Margaret Fullerton Ferguson, who made her debut with 29 other flowers of society at the Galt House last Saturday night. The orchestra played Juanita as her father, Mr. Edward Hite Ferguson, stood at the top of the flower laden grand staircase to escort his daughter down. Miss Jennie C. Benedict, the caterer, provided refreshments on tables covered with Belgian lace and set with Waterford crystal. Miss Gloyer, the seamstress, provided the dress, her latest silk creation, for Miss Margaret."

Although this space is solid and grounded enough, one striking feature on the far wall nonetheless anchors the lobby with its massive proportions and imposing size. Brilliant with its creamy white contrast against the rich woods of the room, a huge Renaissance Revival Caen fireplace – hand-carved as one single piece in France and shipped whole to the United States – hints at the splendor of the Gilded Age.

Edwin Hite Ferguson had married Sophie Fullerton Marfield in a lavish 1898 wedding at the age of 48, and the stone chimneypiece was hand-carved to commemorate their union. The two coats of arms on the mantel represent Mr. and Mrs. Ferguson's respective families, the Ferguson crest on the right bearing the motto Industria, or "diligence," a fitting motto for a business-minded man. The coat of arms to the left belongs to the Fullerton clan of Mrs. Ferguson's mother, and its crest bears the dictum Lux in Tenebris, which translates to "light in darkness." This counts as an appropriate slogan as well, given that today's tenant of the Ferguson Mansion has always been recognized as an important center for the study of the region's history and culture.

Stepping through an entryway to the left, one enters the home's original library, which currently serves as a lounge for members of The Filson. Distinguished by original built-in bookcases, the mansion's library has soaring plaster ceilings and light fixtures custom designed by Louis Comfort Tiffany for the Ferguson home. These overhead lamps were originally electric, whereas the lights along the walls were piped for gas. Since electricity was not always available or reliable in the early 1900s, the gas lamps served as a backup source of light in the event the electric power went out.

Landscapes painted by well-regarded Kentucky artists Charles Harvey Joiner and Carl Christian Brenner adorn the walls of the library. A native of Germany who arrived in Louisville as a young man, Brenner held an annual party in Louisville during which he would auction off his paintings, and it became quite trendy at the time for affluent homes in this area to showcase at least one of his works. To the south, a door gives access to a sunny conservatory, and another ornate fireplace adds to the elegance of the room. When plans for the mansion were drawn up, Ferguson made sure that each room had a fireplace, even though his residence counted as the very first in Louisville to utilize central heating.

When construction on the home began, this novel form of heating had its quirks, and repairs often resulted in lengthy delays. If the furnace failed, the fireplaces offered a dependable alternative for warming the house, as well as added an aesthetic feature to the room.

Like the other first-floor rooms, the dining room, just off the library, boasts yet another dazzling fireplace. Created by the Chicago firm of Orlando Giannini, the stunning glass tile surround has Art Nouveau-inspired detailing that depicts flowering vines creeping over a brick wall. Overhead, an eye-catching wrap-around mural depicts colorful hunting scenes from the German folk tale "Der Freischutz," as hand-painted characters gaze down at the dining table and carved sideboard that survive from the original Ferguson family collection. If no guests had arrived to join them for the evening, Mr. and Mrs. Ferguson would sit down at the enormous table with their daughter to a four-course dinner prepared and served by the kitchen staff.

Although many years have passed since the scions of Old Louisville's heyday sat at the dining room table, the spirit of the Gilded Age is alive and well at the Ferguson Mansion. And it might even be that a solitary specter of a forgone time haunts the lavish spaces of the beautiful Beaux Arts mansion on Millionaires Row. For years, both employees and visitors at The Filson have reported ghostly antics of a mischievous poltergeist by the name of Sally, who it seems has a penchant for books.

"When I used to work up in the stacks on the upper floors," says Lynn Reynolds, a former research assistant who logged in many hours at The Filson in the late 1980s, "I'd always get these creepy feelings like someone was spying on me. But it always happened when I was alone. When other people were around me, it was okay, but when I was all by myself, forget about it! I hated being up there all by myself."

And as would naturally be expected, this odd sensation usually increased exponentially as the sun went down.

"In the winter, when it got dark very early, those were really the worst times," she says. "I was always getting chills and goose bumps, and my heart seemed to race a lot, besides. Always, though, when I was alone. I thought I was being a little skittish at first – because you know how it is with those big old houses, you don't really need to have much of an imagination before things start going bump in the night – but then I started noticing things moving."

When Reynolds asked her coworkers if they had any misgivings about spending time in an old home with a possibly haunted past, they usually met her with blank stares or furrowed brows. "Of course, they're all historians there, so they're naturally going to love anything old," she explains, "so I guess I should have expected the puzzled reactions. What I was really trying to say was: 'Have you ever experienced anything spooky-like in this place, or am I the only one?' I got the impression that people might have laughed at me, had I said anything about what I was sensing and feeling, so I just decided to keep it all to myself."

Reynolds wasn't able to keep the startled shriek to herself, however, when a book jumped from its spot in the Kentucky History Room several days later and struck her on the left shoulder as she walked by. "I was returning several items to the shelves and just happened to be passing by, perfectly minding my own business, when out of the corner of my eye I noticed this large book fall from one of the top shelves and hit me on the shoulder. Of course, it scared the life out of me, so I sort of let out a loud yelp, which caused a librarian to come in from the next room and see what the matter was. This time I wasn't alone."

According to Reynolds, the coworker claimed that the book must have fallen from its perch due to the vibrations produced as she walked by the shelf. "Well, I didn't want to argue with him, so I just said, 'Yes, that must be it' and went about my business. But heck, it's not like I weigh 300 pounds or anything. I'm actually quite petite and tend not to set off too many tremors as I walk by things." To assuage her qualms, Reynolds sauntered by the same shelf several times throughout the remainder of the afternoon, each time altering her gait and the pressure of her steps in a vain attempt to recreate any vibrations that could dislodge wayward books from the cases. "It didn't happen once!" she says, "Not a single vibration or the tiniest bit of movement could I see. Those floors are solid, and it would take a little more than me walking by to make a book fall from the shelf."

Fall might not be the correct word, however, as she discovered several weeks after that.

"Yes, I was still getting the creepy creeps in that place, but for the most part I didn't have any books raining down on me when I was there. Just the weird feeling like someone was lurking in the shadows, watching me from a spot where I couldn't see them. But, then something really frightening happened one night."

According to Reynolds, the club had closed for the evening, and she had stayed after to ready a downstairs room for a reception the next day. "I had finished setting up, so I ran back upstairs to check on things one last time and turn off the lights before I went home. That day, for some reason, I hadn't thought about the weird feelings that had been plaguing me up there, so I really wasn't thinking about that at all as I mounted the steps to the floor above."

Although minor modifications have somewhat altered the appearance of the second-floor spaces, they still exude the elegance of a grander age. The rooms of the former master bedroom suite house the vital statistics documents and the Kentucky history collection, and a room that connects them, the old dressing room, still has the original Tiffany light fixtures with their whimsical dragonfly motif. Known as the Dulaney Room, the main reading room houses a small portion of The Filson's 50,000 volumes and originally made up part of the Ferguson's private living quarters.

As she entered the main reading room, however, Reynolds says the atmosphere changed.

"The air felt sort of heavy and electrified, and I felt a sensation of pressure in my chest. So, I just decided to turn off the lights quick and then skedaddle on out of there." But something prevented her from leaving the room as quickly as anticipated. "I was heading to the doorway to make my exit, but as I approached it and one of the bookcases to my right, the most startling thing happened." Reynolds says she watched as a large volume with red-leather binding lifted itself off the topmost shelf, arced through the air and landed on the floor right in front of her.

"It was as if an invisible hand had reached up and grabbed the book from its spot, and then tossed it to the floor. It did not fall from the shelf, I can assure you that, because it was moving too slowly at first. It just sort of floated and hovered in the air. And in addition, when things fall, they do not tend to fall upwards, as had happened with that book when it came out of the shelf at first." But there was more to come.

"And then it happened again to the next book in the row. And the next one after that. One by one, the whole row of books tumbled to the floor until the top shelf had been totally emptied." Reynolds, now in her sixties, says it looked as if a dissatisfied – and invisible – patron had angrily gone through the books on the shelf, quickly examining the title of each after extracting it from the shelf and then discarding the tome in a heap on the carpeting.

"I bolted from the room, and tried to calm my nerves down-stairs. I wanted to go back and reshelf the books since some of them were quite old, but I decided to get out of there and go on home. I locked up and made sure I was the first one there the next morning so I could put them back in their rightful spots. Fortunately, they were still heaped in a little mound on the floor when I came in the next day. If they had been put back, I would have thought I was going crazy."

When her coworker, the librarian who had helped her explain away the previous incident with the jumping book, came in a couple of hours later, Reynolds quickly called him over to her desk and told him about the strange happenings.

"I assumed he wouldn't take it seriously, as he had done before, but you know what? He really listened and nodded his head in encouragement as I recounted what I had witnessed. When I was finished, he shook his head a bit and claimed that he had been having similar experiences as of late." Although he hadn't actually witnessed any books sailing in mid-air, the man alleged that he had on several occasions heard a loud thud as he passed various shelves. Turning around, he had found books lying on the ground behind him. Most of them had been sandwiched securely between other volumes, so it apparently required some force to dislodge them from their positions.

"I really felt better then, because I knew for a fact that I wasn't going crazy. But then he told me something else that he had been experiencing," says Reynolds. "He told me not only had he been having weird things happen with the books, but also he had been smelling strange odors. He claimed there seemed to be a strong whiff of sulfur on more than one occasion. That was a new one on me."

Whereas many experts in the paranormal would more often

than not associate the malodorous presence of sulfur with an entity of demonic nature, Reynolds immediately came up with a different explanation. During a recent spate of research, she had uncovered an interesting bit of information regarding the personal hygiene habits of Margaret, the Ferguson's pampered daughter, and this thought came to mind as Reynolds listened to her librarian friend. "I sort of got the goose bumps because I had found out that Margaret used to like to refresh her skin with water from St. Patrick's Well. They bottled it from a spring just down the block a bit, and because it was so high in mineral content, everyone said it smelled just awful, like sulfur or rotten eggs."

When Reynolds shared this knowledge with her coworker, she says he gave her an incredulous look. "I could really tell that it freaked him out a bit. He just shook his head and said 'seriously?' and then he walked away like he had to reconsider things."

If he ever had a change of heart, Reynolds' colleague never mentioned it during their remaining time at The Filson. "He ended up getting a different job, and not too long after he left, I ended up leaving as well. He was the only person I felt I could confide in, so I never told anyone else about the strange things I witnessed while I was still working there."

Reynolds says her strange encounter with the paranormal would culminate with several additional book incidents before she left the employ of The Filson. "I had about two weeks to go before I quit, and the weird things had sort of abated for a while. I'm not quite sure why, but it was early spring, and I think that the fact that we were so busy and were always having people in the mansion and up in the stacks might have had something to do with it. I could have just been too busy to pay attention to those kinds of things."

In any case, Reynolds found herself alone on the second floor one April evening around 10 o'clock. "We had just put on a lecture about the history of the Ohio River valley, and the people had cleared out and the other employees had all gone home. I was just walking through the place checking on things before I locked everything up for the night. I wasn't expecting anything out of the ordinary to happen."

However, as she approached a shelf of books in the Dulaney Room, she jumped back, a startled witness as a row of books flew from a top shelf and sailed halfway across the room. "These books didn't just fall from the shelf," she says. "The whole row of books came flying off the shelf one by one in rapid succession, starting from one end until there were no more books left, and then they hurled themselves to the long table in the middle of the room. It was as if someone behind the shelf was watching me coming and forcefully knocked the books out at me one at a time to startle me. If I hadn't jumped out of the way, most of them would have struck me. And they were moving fast."

Reynolds then ran from the room and decided to let someone else clean up the mess the next day. "I didn't care. I just wanted to get out of there and not have anything else happen. I was starting to get scared now, so I went home. When I got in the next morning, one of the interns had found the books scattered all over the table, and some on the floor, and he asked me what had happened. I just said I didn't know anything about it."

Although she exercised caution during her last few days with The Filson, Reynolds claimed she wasn't able to leave without one final, disconcerting encounter with the mischievous spirit that allegedly haunts the Ferguson Mansion. Another workday had come and gone, and once again, Reynolds happened to be by herself on the second floor. "There was a custodian busy down in the lower level, but other than that, I was alone again. I only had two days to go, so I was just crossing my fingers that nothing too weird would happen before I was out of there."

No such luck. She had just exited a room where the tables had been pushed up against the wall to facilitate vacuuming, and when she came back to the room a minute or two later, she was in for a shock. "OK. I walked out of the room to return a file to my desk in an adjacent room, and I know there was nothing on the floor as I left. But when I came back into the room, I just stopped dead in my tracks and froze." There, in front of her, a huge letter S had been laid out on the rug in the middle of the floor, the S having been fashioned out of books from the surrounding shelves.

"The breath just caught in my throat, and I almost passed out. Seriously, I started to get light-headed and really felt faint, and it took all I had not to fall over. And there was an odd feeling in the room again.

Almost like I was in a stuffy sauna, but the air was ice cold instead of hot. It was very cold and dense, and that's the only way I can describe the atmosphere." Slowly, Reynolds backed out of the room and hurried to the landing at the top of the stairs.

"I screamed at the top of my lungs for the janitor to come upstairs, but he couldn't hear me, so I finally ran down to get him. I dragged him up the stairs to see it, and I'm sure he must have thought I'd lost my mind because I was frantic. When I pointed to that big S in the middle of the floor and asked if he had done it, he just shook his head back and forth and gave me a wide-eyed look. Of course, I knew he hadn't done it, but I had to ask to make myself feel better. I really wanted there to be a rational explanation."

With the help of the startled man who had been unceremoniously uprooted from his task in the basement, Reynolds says she searched the sprawling house to see if an unknown visitor had managed to enter the building or if some unaccounted-for employee had just not gone home as she had assumed.

"But no," she says, "the place was locked up tight as a drum and it was just the two of us there. I was just glad the books were still laid out in the strange pattern when I took the janitor up there, because I'd have felt the fool if I had dragged him up there for no reason. When we got to talking, I realized that he didn't think I was crazy, so that was a nice reassurance. I asked him if he had ever seen anything strange like that in the house, and he admitted that he hadn't, but he did say he was always hearing footsteps and voices when he was there alone, which was several times a week, late at night. That made me feel better, although I did feel sorry for him having to be there by himself so much."

The down-to-earth custodian, however, seemed to take it all in stride. When Reynolds prompted him to see if he had any ideas of who or what might be haunting the large home, he replied that he always assumed it to be the ghost of Sally, whoever that happened to be. "I quizzed him to see what he knew about the history of the place," says Reynolds, "but he had never heard of anyone by that name living there. He didn't have a plausible explanation for a Sally haunting the place, either."

Although she still felt unnerved, Reynolds felt somewhat secure knowing the custodian would keep her company in the house as she picked up the books from the floor and returned them to their shelves. "He went back downstairs and I started collecting them. I counted them, and there were over forty of them, all of them taken from the top shelves of the two nearest bookcases. And the strange thing was how neatly they had been laid out end to end to form that big letter S."

On a whim, Reynolds says she gathered up an armful of books after the giant S had been cleared away and tried to recreate the pattern in the same spot on the floor. "And you know what? I got it to look like an S all right, but it wasn't anything like the one I had found there. That one was a perfect shape, with all the edges coming together seamlessly to make a nice, solid letter. Mine didn't even come close. Weird, huh?"

Two days later, Reynolds left The Filson. She hasn't returned to the lavish mansion since. "I'm just glad nothing else happened after the S-thing," she says, "because I don't think I could have handled it. I've talked to someone there in the meantime, and he said there are occasional reports of odd noises and shadowy forms, but nothing as strange as what I experienced, from what I can tell."

Although various reports of would-be paranormal activity at the old Ferguson Mansion have surfaced throughout the years, most do not consider it a hotbed of ghostly phenomena. Rather, many see it as a venerable structure that has graced Old Louisville's Millionaires Row for more than a century, and as such, it is bound to have associated with it the normal retinue of legend and lore that come with the passage of time. When a blustery wind rails against the gathering darkness outside, the myriad creaks and groans that naturally accompany an older home often tend to morph into spectral footsteps and hair-raising visits from the netherworld. I'm sure it's no different in the lovely Ferguson Mansion.

However, accounts like that of Lynn Reynolds do make one stop and think. And, she's not the only person who has reported eerie goings-on at the Beaux Arts residence on Third Street.

Lydia Harris, a local historian, has spent many hours in the mansion conducting research for various articles she has published about early Kentucky pioneers and settlers. On more than one occasion, she's been an unwilling witness to random books that have fallen to her feet while roaming the second floor in search of old documents and out-of-print books. "Not that I believe in ghosts or anything," she explains, "but there have been some strange things in that place – usually involving books. I can't remember the number of times I'd be up on the second floor when a book would just fall off the shelf and land at my feet as I walked by. I've even had it take place when others were in the room with me, and they just seemed to think it was something that happened now and then. No one seemed to worry about it too much, so I didn't let it bother me, either."

But Harris recalls one occasion that did upset her.

"I was there one morning in early September, and it was a beautiful Indian summer day, so I really didn't want to be inside. But I had to do research to get an article done, so I just decided to stick it out and get it over and done with. I was on the second floor, and strangely enough, no one else was up there. I think they were having a staff meeting or something down in the dining room, so I was all alone. It didn't bother me, though."

That is, until she needed help once she found herself locked in a small room on the second floor. "There was this little room up there, and they had a couple of files with old maps and boxes of microfiche and stuff like that. I went in there to get a notepad I had left behind, and as I turned around to walk back out into the main reading room, the door just slammed shut all by itself. I actually saw it swing to, and there was nobody in sight who could have done that."

When Harris grabbed the door handle and turned it to open the door, she realized that the door had somehow become locked. "Or stuck. It just wouldn't budge. I pulled and turned on the knob, and it wouldn't move at all. It was like the entire door had become part of the wall, and I couldn't even cause it to rattle in its frame. I tried and tried and tried, and finally I just gave up and started to pound on the door to get someone's attention on the outside." But since the sliding doors to the dining room had been closed, her pounding fell on deaf ears.

"After several minutes of that, I'm not ashamed to say I started to panic. I'm a bit claustrophobic, so it didn't help being in a small space like that, either. Finally, I just gathered my wits about me and told myself to calm down and take a break. I knew there were other people in the building, so I just assured myself that someone would find me eventually. I took a deep breath and sat down on one of the two chairs in the room."

At which point the door smoothly and effortlessly swung open, revealing an empty reading room on the other side.

"I started to hear the theme song from the *Twilight Zone* in my head as I ran out of there and went to my spot at the table. I looked around, and it still looked like everyone was still down in the dining room, so I just sat down and convinced myself that it had been a fluke, nothing more." Nonetheless, Harris claims she couldn't shake the feeling of unease for the rest of the day.

"And the strangest thing," she says, "was that when I went to get my things and get back to work, I noticed that someone had written something on the page I had been working on in my notebook." In an elegant, flowing script, a feminine hand had written the name SALLY.

"The hair stood up on the back of my neck. I looked around to see if anyone was there, but the place was still empty. That's when I started to wonder if someone hadn't been pranking me. Stranger things have happened. Maybe one of the employees wanted to perpetuate the legends of the ghost named Sally on the premises. Who knows? I'm convinced I still don't believe in spirits, if there is such a thing, but I still have had some strange things happen to me there."

Others in the Filson have experienced similar encounters with flying books, artful patterns laid out on the floor, odd smells and eerie footsteps, and whenever the question arises as to what the purported cause may be, the answer always leads in one direction: Sally. Never sure as to who Sally might have actually been, most only reply that she's a poltergeist associated with the house and that her antics have become part and parcel of the local history.

Most aficionados of the supernatural understand the German term poltergeist to be synonymous with playful spirits or prank-playing specters, the word translating most accurately as 'noisy ghost' in English. This seems to offer a plausible source for the would-be haunting at The Filson. But whereas some experts claim that a poltergeist aligns itself with or stems from the prepubescent energy of maturing children or teenagers, usually female, this does not seem to be the case with Sally.

No individuals had ever reported incidents revolving around children; spectral activity only seems to happen in the presence of adults, and grounded adults not prone to flights of fancy at that.

As often happens with alleged causes of hauntings that I uncover, I try to find out as much as I can about the previous occupants of a property, as well as research the physical history of the location. With the Ferguson Mansion, this proved to be extremely easy, as documents and articles abound about the first family who resided there. However, there doesn't appear to be a Sally associated with the family or the early years of the sprawling mansion. After poring through pages of family information and interviewing people who knew about the house and its past, I came up empty-handed as far as potential haunts were concerned.

Having lived in an old home myself, I know that strange noises and disconcerting flickers of shadow can wreak havoc on the imagination, especially when you're at home alone, so I just figured that someone had coined the name for the resident spook in the heat of the moment and it had stuck since then. After all, it's much more interesting to blame a misplaced set of keys or an odd series of creaks and groans in an old place on a resident specter than it is on normal, old-home noises or forgetfulness. That's why I concluded that there probably had never been a Sally in the house; she had been concocted out of whimsy and fright and evolved into a coverall for all the purported supernatural events in the mansion and eventually assumed a life of her own, if such can be said for spirits who are, in essence, dead.

But then I took a second look at the history of the huge mansion on Third Street. The Fergusons had been in residence for close to twenty years, but their successors, the Pearsons, had spent even more time at the place. And not only that, they had operated the family business out of the opulent residence until 1978.

The family-run operation? The Pearson Family Funeral Home.

For over five decades, the stately Ferguson Mansion had served as the city's premier undertaker's parlor, an elegant place of final repose for many of Louisville's Gilded Age luminaries. To look at it today, no one would suspect that the beautiful home had devoted more than a half century to the practice of the mortuary sciences, but there are telltale signs that hint at the home's morbid past.

One is in the home's impressive foyer, where the original lobby once culminated in a magnificently carved grand stairway leading to the second and third floors. Although much of the staircase, including the banister, remained intact, the Pearsons altered it to make room for a side entrance to the funeral home, unfortunately removing an impressive stained glass window that scattered random jewels of light over the main entry hall. Another significant modification to the building came with the addition of an elevator – an elevator about eight feet long by four feet wide – with just enough room to transport a casket.

With no historical substantiation from the Ferguson record to bolster the claims of a poltergeist by the name of Sally, I therefore have come to one conclusion: In the fifty-plus years that the mansion catered to the needs of the dearly departed, there had to be at least one Sally among them, a Sally who entered the lavish home as an unfortunate cadaver. And, on seeing the opulent appointments, the gleaming hardwoods, the intricate millwork and inviting fireplaces, this languid spirit decided to postpone its imminent departure from this life for a brief respite in the lap of luxury. Melancholy and world-weary, she lingers as a shadow of her former self amid the trappings of a grander time. Content with solitary nights cavorting in the gloom of the darkened mansion, she amuses herself with a harmless trick every now and then to maintain some connection with the living. A seductive whisper in an unsuspecting ear, a book or two tossed about in jest, a playful arrangement of volumes in the shape of the letter S left out as a sign in the middle of the floor – these are just a few of the ways Sally likes to let people know the Ferguson Mansion belongs to her.

Much of this information was provided courtesy of The Filson Historical Society Web site at www.filsonhistorical.org. The Ferguson Mansion is generally open from 9 a.m. to 5 p.m. weekdays, and visitors are welcome.

ABOUT BOCKEE MANOR

The Ferguson Mansion is not the only residence in the neighborhood that has been used as a funeral parlor. A striking structure at 1230 South Third Street – one that has unfortunately seen better days – provided undertaking services from 1927 to 1938, when Dougherty & Sons located their family business there. It's hardly surprising that rumors abound that a spook or two might haunt the shabby interior of the gray and white residence.

The once stately mansion had already gained some degree of national renown shortly after completion when a correspondent from *Harper's Weekly* included a sketch of it in a pictorial report on the impressive homes springing up in the young city of Louisville. The original owner, James Bockee, a wealthy banker and partner in the prestigious firm of Bockee, Garth & Schroeder Leaf Tobacco, had the dwelling built at the close of the Southern Exposition in 1887. It was a year that saw the addition of many new mansions to the burgeoning Millionaires Row, and Bockee Manor, as it came to be known, attracted no small amount of admiration with its elegant keyhole entry and rooftop balcony tucked away in a lattice-trimmed dormer. Bockee and his family enjoyed a comfortable life there for more than a dozen years before the building became home to a series of subsequent renters and owners, including Dougherty & Sons. Not long after the Dougherty family vacated the premises, rumors started circulating that the spirits of dead bodies that had spent their last few days above ground in the flower-laden parlors of the funeral home had decided to linger on in a more ethereal form.

Although nobody has come forward with first-hand accounts of actual encounters with these alleged ghosts, stories persist that the old mansion is populated with specters. Its days as a funeral parlor seem to have imprinted the old house with a negative stereotype that subsequently resulted in a haunted reputation.

Whether or not ghosts actually haunt the old Bockee Manor, neighbors insist nonetheless that some scary things are going on there. However, these allegations don't involve reports of disembodied spirits and spectral voices. Rather, their suspicions entail a simple dissatisfac-

Once an architectural gem of Old Louisville's Millionaires Row, the former residence of tobacco baron J.S. Bockee has fallen on hard times.

tion with recent tenants who have proved to be less than perfect neighbors since a recent owner gutted much of the bottom floor and started leasing the property. For years, the building housed the Kentucky Barber College, and its steady stream of noisy students and local panhandlers in search of free haircuts proved to be a bone of contention with other residents on the block. And not too long ago, a children's daycare center moved in and compounded the problems. Although many assumed that loud children would prove to be a regular source of annoyance, it wasn't the case. Rather, it was the inconsiderate parents dropping off and picking up the children who ended up disturbing residents with their booming car stereos, loud yelling and penchant for littering. Some neighbors would rather have the ghosts.

ABOUT KENTUCKY'S
FIRST EMBALMER

Edward C. Pearson held the first embalmer's license issued in the state and became a leader in promoting the education and licensing of embalmers. The son of Pearson family patriarch Lorenzo Dow Pearson, Edward designed an original wood paneled hearse, the body of which was later mounted on a motor-driven chassis to create Louisville's first motorized hearse. Early on, funeral processions for Louisville's wealthiest citizens often entailed a high degree of ceremony and elaborate attention to detail. Many of the cavalcades organized by Edward Pearson featured highly polished, lacquered interment carriages drawn by raven-hued horses bedecked in coal-black plumes and crepe. Brass bands playing dirges often followed behind and provided a steady stream of mournful tunes to the cemetery. With the advent of the automobile, these regal horse-drawn funeral processions soon disappeared, and garages replaced the stables at Pearson's place of business. Many of Old Louisville's most prominent citizens of the Gilded Age arrived at their final resting place in ceremonial splendor thanks to the work of Edward Pearson.

ABOUT THE OLD FILSON CLUB

In the spring of 1884, a number of prominent Louisvillians gathered at the home of Reuben T. Durrett and established The Filson Historical Society to honor Kentucky's first historian, John Filson. One of Kentucky's earliest settlers, Filson enjoyed renown for his cartographic efforts that resulted in the first comprehensive map of the state. In addition, his book, *The Discovery, Settlement, and Present State of Kentucke*, established his reputation as the foremost historian in the

The primary founder and first president of The Filson Historical Society, Reuben T. Durrett, lived on Breckinridge Street in a house that would grow into the first headquarters of the esteemed organization.

area. The oldest, privately supported historical society in the state, The Filson has evolved and grown since its inception in the library of Durrett's house and now counts as one of the most significant institutions in the region. Its mission is the collection and preservation of significant stories associated with the history and culture of Kentucky and the Ohio River valley.

Although it moved to its current location in the 1980s, the building where The Filson Historical Society got its start still stands today at 118 West Breckinridge Street. The 19th-century structure underwent a serious makeover in previous years when workers attached it to the adjacent house and then added on a third floor, but the spirit of early Kentucky history reportedly lives on in the original rooms. Some even believe that the spirits of early Kentucky historians might live on in the former chambers of the old Durrett home.

The DeMuth family acquired the property in the 1980s, and today they operate a successful advertising agency from the premises, along with several other family-run enterprises. More than one of the employees on the grounds have reported spectral encounters in the past. For example, Mike Sales, a former custodian, claims a ghostly vision greeted him late one evening in the front entry hall of the building. "I saw this man holding a book just walk out of the doorway to the left of me. He just stopped in front of the door and appeared to read a bit. Then he disappeared. I thought it was very strange. Not because he disappeared just like that, but also because he appeared to be wearing clothes from the 1800s."

Others have reported similar sightings over the years, and most seem to involve scholarly specters – some of them even sporting spectacles – with opened books in their hands. The building at one time served as a local school, so there could reasonably be a number of scholarly types associated with the past lives of the old Filson Club. But, what actually – if anything – lurks in the shadows of the unassuming structure on West Breckinridge has yet to be determined.

Chapter 2

THE BOWEN HOUSE

Sheltered by towering shade trees, a unique building sits on the 1300 block of South Third Street. I walk by it every day with my dogs, and it is one of those unusual buildings that have always piqued my curiosity. Like so many of the homes in Old Louisville, red brick figures prominently in the construction, something that hearkens back to a day when only the well-to-do could afford residences built of brick and stone. A brightly painted turret juts out from the corner to the north, and two neat porches trimmed in gingerbread – one set back slightly from the other – flank the front of the building. Parallel walkways lead from the street and end at twin sets of steps that go up to the porches, where strange things have been known to happen when the sun goes down and the gas lamps bathe the streets of Old Louisville in a warm glow.

Like so many of the historic structures in Old Louisville, the building at 1324 and 1326 South Third Street harbors a secret. It's not one of those dark, menacing secrets that hides a long-lost murder or covers up evil deeds, but rather one of a more mundane nature. It's the kind of secret that involves nothing more than the all-too-common themes of family intrigue and sibling rivalry.

The story has it that construction on the spacious home began sometime around 1890, when Mr. E.H. Bowen, a well-to-do merchant,

An early example of an Old Louisville duplex, the Bowen House is the location of a local haunt known as "the old lady in the rocking chair."

decided to build a "semi-detached" home on Third Avenue's emerging Millionaires Row. Although one might still hear that term in use in England today, it has fallen out of vogue in this country, and most opt for the more accepted "duplex" when referring to a two-family home here. As can be imagined, this reportedly caused more than a little consternation among the well-heeled residents of Third Avenue, who balked at anything other than the notion of a three-story, single-family mansion joining their ranks. The respectable, albeit nouveau riche, families of the area had to have their own homes and grounds, and people who didn't meet these rigid standards lived "beneath" them. God forbid anyone should talk of apartment living, a maverick lifestyle for those off-kilter dwellers content with "living life on a shelf" or "packed in the sardine can." And on Millionaires Row at least, residing in semi-detached homes was only one notch above apartment living.

When word got out about Bowen's duplex, resistance – if not in the neighborhood, along Third Avenue – arose to foil his plans for the structure. It was rumored that some of his prospective neighbors had even threatened to take Bowen to court in an effort the thwart the addition of the two-family home in the burgeoning single-family streetscape of Millionaires Row. That was until the reason for Bowen's building the duplex came to light. Mr. Bowen, it would seem, was encumbered with two daughters who had entered their 30s as single women. Society at that time relegated the two ladies to irrevocable spinsterhood, and their father had no choice but to provide them with a comfortable abode in which to live out their remaining years.

Whether it was this revelation that softened the steely resolve of the Third Avenue residents or the fact that Bowen's financial situation had recently revealed him to be wealthier than most of his Old Louisville neighbors, nobody can say. But a wave of charity nonetheless swept the barren lot at what would become 1324 and 1326 South Third Street, and the community welcomed the Bowen sisters with open arms. Mr. Bowen had the home built, and the sisters moved in, each taking up residence in her half of the dwelling.

For many years, so the story goes, the sisters lived in their comfortable home.

When the last spinster passed away as the Great Depression loomed on the Kentucky horizon, new owners moved in and, within years, the Bowen sisters of Third Avenue were all but forgotten.

But about that time, the first reports of strange occurrences on the front porches started circulating throughout the neighborhood.

Unexplained apparitions and odd, bouncing balls of orange light in the air began manifesting themselves on the front porches, usually in the warm evenings of the spring and summer. According to numerous eyewitnesses, they were eerie, glowing orbs of light that would dance back and forth between one porch to the other.

"It was about 8 in the evening," says Norbert Samuels, an Old Louisville resident who recalls a particular evening in the late 1930s as he strolled along Third Street with his mother, "and we were passing by the old Bowen place." Samuels and his mother lived in a small apartment on nearby Kentucky Street, and they – like many in the area – had acquired the habit of taking regular after-dinner strolls. This, no doubt, harkened back to the early days when Third Street, originally named Third Avenue, counted as the main promenade thoroughfare in the city. Clad in the latest fashions, Old Louisvillians of the Gilded Age considered a stroll down its wide sidewalks an essential part of every Sunday afternoon. And an evening walk or "constitutional" down what the locals simply referred to as "the Street" would become a tradition that lasted until the years after World War II when city dwellers started fleeing to the suburbs.

"It was a beautiful spring evening," says Samuels, "and the light was just beginning to fade, when all of a sudden my mother stopped abruptly." Samuels, who would have been no more than five at the time, recalls that her grip on his hand tightened as she turned and stared at the porch. "I wasn't really paying attention at first, so I just stood there. But after I realized that she was looking at something, I looked up and followed her gaze to the porch on the old Bowen place."

The young Samuels drew in close to his mother as he squinted his eyes to make out the activity on the porch. "There was a bouncing light or something there, and that's what had caught her attention," the now 80-year-old recalls. "Today I know it would have been called a light orb, but back then it just looked like a shiny pin prick bouncing around. It was kind of yellowish orange and very bright. I'd never seen anything like it." Samuels says that he and his mother stood for several minutes and observed as the orb darted back and forth across the porch. "It just kept bouncing back and forth, and then it sort of exploded and turned into a gray see-through cloud." Samuels says he then heard a gasp from his mother, which caused him to turn and look. "She raised the other hand to her mouth, and when I turned back to look at the porch, I saw why."

According to Samuels, the cloud had assumed the shape of what appeared to be an old woman sitting in a rocking chair.

"She looked like she had white hair done up in a bun in the back, and she was just sitting in a rocking chair, rocking back and forth," he says. "My mother and I talked about it for years afterwards, and that's when we finally realized that other people had seen the same thing." The ghost of the old lady in the rocking chair, as she came to be known, had apparently become a permanent fixture on Third Street.

"As children, our parents always used to tell us about the ghosts in the neighborhood," recalls Annabel Jordan, a Fourth Street resident who grew up in the very house her grandparents built in the late 1800s. "And of all the stories we would hear, I always loved hearing about the old lady in the rocking chair. It wasn't a scary story at all. That's what I liked about it. It was just a nice old lady people would see every now and then." Little did Annabel Jordan know that she would one day be one of those people to witness the apparition of the old dame in the rocking chair.

"I remember the night quite well," recalls the 69-year-old math teacher "because I had just left my best friend's birthday party and was on my way home from the corner of Third and Gaulbert. She had just turned ten, and it was May 5, 1949." Jordan says nothing seemed out of the ordinary as she walked down the brick sidewalk and approached the house to her left. "That's what I thought at first," she recalls, "but then something caught my eye. There was some kind of form on the porch. It was gray and cloudy." Once she reached the first walkway leading up to the front steps, Jordan says she stopped and tried to focus on the vague shape before her. "I wanted to go up the walkway and get closer to the porch, but something in the back of my head told me to stay put. Maybe it was because the hair was standing up on the back of my arms."

The young girl stood there for a full minute and tried to make sense of what she was seeing. "It was very faint, but there was a definite shape on the stoop. I knew right away I had to be seeing the ghost of the old lady in the rocking chair because I could see right through the apparition to the brick wall on the other side of her. I had never seen such a thing!" After a moment or two studying the strange sight, Jordan says she could even make out distinguishing features on the ghost. "It looked like it was sitting in an old-fashioned, high-back rocker, and I could see her hair in a bun on the back of her head. There also appeared to be a white, long-sleeved blouse with a cameo brooch at the collar and high-top, black leather boots. I could even see that she had on a pair of small, wire-framed spectacles."

Not too long after the realization that she had come across the apparition of the famed old lady in the rocking chair, Jordan says the ghostly form simply disappeared. "Just like that," she explains, "it vanished! There one second and gone the next! In all my life I had never experienced such an odd encounter. I won't forget it until the day I die."

Others who have experienced first-hand the ghost of the old lady in the rocking chair share this sentiment. "I never saw her myself," says Richard Oswald, a former resident of Old Louisville who now resides in San Diego, "but I can vividly recall both my grandmother and grandfather talking about her. Both of them claimed to have seen her in the 40s when they were both kids. The thing that I recall most is them saying that they could see that she was wearing glasses, the old-fashioned kind that looked like little round spectacles."

Ruth Gibson remembers the same kind of glasses on the nose of the specter she spied in the 1950s when she and her older brother would spend summers with their grandparents in a palatial home on Ormsby Avenue. "They had the most amazing house, and I'm pretty sure it's still in good shape, even though it was divided into apartments in the 1960s. The grand staircase was the most striking feature of the home, and I have many fond memories playing on it as child. There was an absolutely huge landing between the second and first floors with an incredible stained-glass window. It was gorgeous."

Gibson says it was on this same landing with the large stained-glass window where she first heard tell of the old lady in the rocking chair. "My brother and I used to go up there at night and tell ghost stories. We'd wait until right after the sun went down; we'd grab a flashlight and blanket and go up there after dinner to see who could scare the other more. Rance, my brother, usually won." Years later, Ruth Gibson says the story that she remembers most vividly is that of the lady in the rocking chair.

"The way my brother told it was that an old woman was sitting out on her porch one night and an escaped convict found her and murdered her, and that's why her ghost still haunts the spot. But it turns out that he was really exaggerating the story. There wasn't a murder at all. Leave it to my brother to try and make the story gorier than it actually was."

However, Gibson didn't discover this fact till many years later, many years after she had a strange encounter with the apparition herself.

"It was the summer of 1955, and we only had a week left at my grandparents," she recalls. "It was the Thursday before Labor Day weekend, and the last thing on my mind was ghosts. I spent the day with a girlfriend at her house down by the university and I was just walking home down Third when I looked up and saw a strange light out of the corner of my eye." At that moment, Gibson realized that she found herself in front of the mysterious porches at 1324 and 1326 South Third Street.

"I swear, just a couple nights before, my brother had been telling me about the ghost of the old woman in the rocking chair, and all of a sudden, there I was in front of the porch he had been telling me about. And there was this strange little ball of light, just sort of dancing around." According to Gibson, the orb seemed to float in the air, bouncing back and forth between the two porches that flanked the front of the house.

"At first I thought it was a reflection from somewhere," she explains, "but after studying it for a bit, I realized it couldn't have been a reflection. I could see that it had some dimension to it. It was spherical in shape." After what seemed to be a minute or two, Gibson says that the point of light exploded before her eyes.

"It erupted into a little cloud of sparkling light with all these little shimmering bits. It's very hard to explain, but that's what happened. All of a sudden there was this cloud hanging there, and the light sort of faded away. At first I couldn't believe my eyes and thought I had to be imagining it or something. Or that there had to be some explanation for it."

But Ruth Gibson didn't have an explanation for what happened next.

"Believe it or not, the cloud started to increase in size, and it gradually began contracting and expanding and changing its shape. People think I'm crazy when I tell them this story, but it eventually assumed the shape of what looked like an old woman sitting in a rocking chair. I swear it. You could even see her rocking back and forth."

Ruth Gibson says she stood there for another half minute or so. Then the mysterious figure faded from sight and vanished.

"It was as if she had never been there at all! I looked around to see if there was anybody in the vicinity who could corroborate what I had just seen, but I was alone. No one was on the porch. It was just me and my chill bumps."

She scratched her head and reluctantly made her way home.

"Of course, I wanted to tell my brother," she explains, "but I had the sneaking suspicion that he wouldn't believe me." Although he enjoyed telling ghost stories, it appears that her older brother didn't necessarily believe in specters himself. "Tom loved scaring me and all, but he was very much the scientific kind," says Gibson. "For him, there had to be a rational explanation for everything, or else it didn't count. The only explanation for ghosts in his mind came from the paranormal, so he dismissed the idea of ghosts as reality. It was just fun and games in the end, and that's what he enjoyed."

It turns out her suspicions weren't entirely unfounded. When she arrived at her grandparent's large home on Ormsby Avenue, she rushed upstairs to tell her brother what she had witnessed.

"He just sort of looked at me like I was crazy," she confides. "He didn't accuse me of lying or anything, but I could tell he didn't believe what I was telling him. He said I must have seen an odd reflection or something, or that someone had to be playing a prank on me. He still says that to this day. Even though he has talked to other people who claim to have seen the very same thing, he remains the eternal skeptic."

But when it comes to the ghost of the old lady in the rocking chair, there are skeptics who have been swayed.

One of them is Madeline Hecht. She has become a firm believer in the specter that haunts the porches at the late Victorian duplex in the heart of Old Louisville. She is also the person who shared some very interesting information that might explain the reason for the purported haunting.

"I used to live in that building," she explains. "I'm related to the Armstrongs, who at one time lived there. They were real bigwigs in the neighborhood and had quite a lot of money at one time. They got involved with the telephone when it first came out in Louisville and made a killing from it." John Armstrong, president of the Louisville Home Telephone Company, would eventually move out of the home and purchase a much grander residence just a half block down the street. "I think most of the strange stuff with ghosts on the porch started way after they moved out," says Hecht, "so I doubt that they ever heard any of the weird stories. But when I lived there some forty years ago, most of the people I knew in the neighborhood had heard about the little old lady who would return from the grave every now and then to rock a spell on her front porch."

An amateur historian who has lived most her life in the Old Louisville neighborhood, Hecht says she considered herself a skeptic when she first heard the accounts of odd specters in rocking chairs plaguing the front porch of the duplex at 1324 and 1326 South Third Street. "I'm pretty straight-laced," she explains, "and I had always been told there were no such things as ghosts. My father was a science teacher, and my mother was an atheist, so neither of them believed in the eventuality of an afterlife. For them, specters were nothing more than the result of an over-active imagination."

But Hecht says she always had a fascination with old homes and ghost stories. "I didn't believe in ghosts per se since I had never seen anything, but I still loved to read about ghosts and hear other people's stories about encounters with them. I don't know what it was, but I really loved ghost stories." And when she heard the odd tale about the old lady in the rocking chair that supposedly haunted the front porch where she lived, it quickly became one of her favorite ghost stories.

"When I lived there, there was an Irish woman who would come in from Butchertown once a week and clean the place for us," she explains. "Her name was Mary, and she was highly superstitious. So it didn't surprise me at all that she believed in ghosts and would tell me stories all the time. In fact, I think she got a rise out of telling me those stories and trying to scare me." Mary, as it turns out, would also be the first individual to give Madeline Hecht a first-hand account of the strange activity that frequented her front stoop.

"One day, Mary came in from a bad storm outside. She was sort of flustered as she shook the water from her umbrella and asked me if I had seen her. When I asked her who she was talking about she just sort of looked at me like I was crazy and shook her head. 'The old woman in the rocking chair, that's who' was her answer. This time I was the one who looked at her like she was crazy."

According to the older woman, a foggy shape resembling that of a woman sitting in a rocking chair had just vanished from the porch. "She told me she had just walked up the front steps and was collapsing her umbrella when she looked up and saw the form to her right." Although the apparition had a somewhat hazy cast to it, the startled woman claims she could still make out enough features on the specter to identify it as an elderly woman with grayish hair done up in a bun in the back. "And she even said it was wearing glasses – the old-fashioned, round spectacle type – and a high-waisted skirt to boot. Now, I don't know if she was telling the truth or not, but she did seem sincere at the time of recounting. Like I said, she was always making things up to scare me, so she could have been inventing this time, too. But I found it strange that she was reporting the types of things on the ghost that people had been talking about before. Who knows? Maybe she was just repeating what she had heard from other people."

But there was no such explanation for the sight that greeted Hecht's eyes one morning in April as she knelt in the front yard and pulled weeds from the flower bed while her mother prepared lunch inside. "It was just your average cool spring morning, and I was enjoying myself among the jonquils and pansies, praying that my mother wasn't preparing chipped beef on toast for me. To this day, that is something I simply cannot abide."

Hecht says she heard something stir on the porch and averted her gaze there, mesmerized by what she saw. "I looked up, and there she was! Just as plain as the nose on your face. It was an old lady in a rocking chair, gently rocking back and forth, and it didn't even look like she noticed I was there. She did seem a bit one-dimensional to me – sort of like an old black-and-white newspaper photograph – but it was clearly the ghost I had heard talk about." As with other sightings, Hecht says the apparition sported a bun in the back, small wire-framed spectacles and a long-sleeved, old-fashioned blouse with a cameo and lace at the throat.

"But that's all I was able to make out," she explains, "because as soon as I saw her, I yelled for my mother and ran inside. And you would have thought someone had gotten themselves killed by the way I was screaming! My mother almost had a heart attack when I ran to the kitchen. I was just all over the place, trying to grab her hand to get her to come back with me to the front porch.

"But, of course, by the time I finally dragged her out there, there was nothing to be seen. When I was able to get my wits about me and tell her what I had seen, she just gave me that kind of look that all kids hate getting from their parents: a pitying stare that said she didn't believe me and might have even been disappointed by me. No amount of pleading could convince her that I was telling the truth. It really bothered me, too, because my mother knew I was not the kind of child to make things up.

"Fortunately, my mother finally gave in and conceded that I must have seen something, however, she would never admit that I saw a ghost, always claiming that I had to have seen a strange reflection or else some kind of hallucination. That was my mother for you. Till the day she died, she would not entertain the notion of anything possible in the afterlife."

Hecht says that this was the case even after she came up with a plausible explanation for the haunting on the porch.

"We ended up moving out of there several years after I saw the ghost, but from that point on, I was obsessed about finding out who the ghost was. My mother being the rational being that she was, I figured I needed proof of some sort. So I started talking to people and tracking down different reports of ghostly sightings on the porch. I was sure if I could prove that someone fitting that description lived there, my mother would be more prone to accept it.

"I talked to two people who had seen her, and they described the exact same thing I had seen, so that wasn't really of any help, other than in the sense that it turned out to be something that corroborated my initial sighting. When I asked them if they knew anything about who or what the ghost was, none of them had an answer.

"That's when I decided to start talking to the old-timers in the neighborhood and see what people knew about the house and all the different families who had lived there. At first, it was slow going, and it didn't seem that I would find anyone who knew anything. I talked to several elderly people who had spent their entire lives in this area, and one of them said he knew of two older women who had lived in the house at one time, but he said he didn't remember either of them wearing their hair up in a bun like that. From what he said, it seems they were both pretty big women and had darker hair – not thin like the specter I had seen, and not having gray or white hair. That's when I sort of gave up and stopped asking people so many questions.

"But then one day – out of the blue – I met someone who had an interesting story to tell. It was in October, the cold weather was just around the corner, and my parents had hired a painter to come and touch up the wood trim on the porch and the windows. I guess I've always been a talker, because I spent most of the day outside watching the painter and chewing his ear off. Looking back, I'm sure he must have been extremely annoyed by all my questions, but if he was, he never showed it. He was a nice old guy and patiently answered all my questions, never giving the impression that he was bored.

"In any case, I ended up asking him a ton of questions about painting and the kind of paint and tools he was using, and the conversation eventually took a turn to talking about the house and the kind of architecture it had. It seems that back then people didn't appreciate the old Victorian homes as much as they do now, and a lot of people thought the houses in Old Louisville were old-fashioned, dark and gloomy, nothing special, but you could tell that this old guy really loved the old homes. He started telling me how hard it was to find nice homes with that quality of construction, and then he started talking about the front porches on the place.

"He told me that ours and the neighboring porch were wonderful examples of Victorian craftsmanship. He started using different terms for the patterns and told me the different names of the various pieces, and, they were, of course, words I had never heard before. And, of course, I don't remember any of them today. But that's when a question came to me. Since he knew so much, I asked him why the porches on the house were the way they were – why one was offset and set farther back than the other. That's when he gave me an answer that gave me goose bumps.

"He stopped what he was doing for a moment and turned to me and said 'Oh. Haven't you heard that story? There used to be two old sisters who lived here – one on this side and the other one on the other side – and they didn't get along well. They supposedly refused to live next to each other; that's how much they disliked each other. So, their father built them each a separate porch so they would be able to sit outside in their rocking chairs and not have to look at each other!'

"Then he just turned around and went back to painting, not understanding the shock he had just delivered. The hair just stood up on my arms and the back of my neck. I didn't know what to say, so I just went back inside and sat on my bed, thinking about it all for a while. That was the connection I needed to explain the haunting, but when I eventually told my mother, she didn't pay me no never-mind, although I did notice the strange look she got on her face when I told her what I had learned. To this day, I think deep down she must have wondered a bit if my story couldn't have been true after all."

The many individuals who have had personal encounters with the specter known as the old lady in the rocking chair no doubt believe the story to be true. But, as is so often the case with these kinds of tales, no concrete proof exists that two feuding elderly sisters inhabited the red brick duplex at 1324 and 1326 South Third Street. I had my friend John Schuler pull up the deeds to the property, and he was able to confirm that a family by the name of Bowen owned the property early on. Belle Booker Bowen, the wife of E. H. Bowen, can be found on one of the early deeds, but other than that, no mention is made of other Bowen family members. When she died, her widower inherited the residence, so if there were any children, it is very plausible that they could have lived on in the property while it was still in their father's name. But until proof emerges that substantiates the existence of the two unnamed Bowen sisters, aficionados of Old Louisville ghost stories will have to wonder if the story of the old lady in the rocking chair draws more heavily on fact or fiction. In all likelihood, the tale has evolved as a combination of both, making it a colorful legend with a basis in history. In the research I've done, I did find one mention of this story in an old walking tour brochure of the neighborhood, but other than that, no written evidence exists.

One day, as I was walking the dogs past the old Bowen place, I couldn't resist. So I tied up the dogs and snuck up to the front porch at 1326. I stood where I imagined an old rocker most likely would have been placed and looked out toward the street. I glanced to the side and then ran over to the porch at 1324 and did the same thing. Staring out at the traffic making its way south on Third Street, I glanced back over at the porch where I had just been, and sure enough, I could see it was true: When you were on one porch, you had no view of what was happening on the other porch. If two quarrelsome siblings had indeed lived at this address, it would have been very possible to sit out at night and have no contact with the other.

ABOUT THE ARMSTRONG MANSION

One of the largest residences on the Millionaires Row, the former home of Mrs. John A. Armstrong, sits at 1359 South Third Street. Constructed in 1899, it had all the trappings of a modern home looking toward the conveniences of the 20th century. Steam radiators, state-of-the-art electrical wiring and an in-house cooling system made it the envy of many in the region. "It is one of the most beautiful and original dwelling houses in the city," wrote the *Courier-Journal* of the Clark and Loomis masterpiece on January 28, 1900. "In a modified Renaissance style in design, but exact in detail, it excites admiration at once. The material is pressed brick, of Roman pattern, with Lake Superior red sandstone trimmings. The portion, with solid side-entrance steps, is a

The Armstrong Mansion, circa 1899, once one of the most glorious homes on Old Louisville's Millionaires Row.

beautiful feature, also the symmetrical swells and double bays on the front. The high-pitch roof gives a rather picturesque and not incongruous effect, which the alcove over the central window is an odd but acceptable trimming."

The Armstrongs occupied the mansion until sometime after 1910, when it passed to the hands of the Hert family, and in the 1930s it served a stint as the Carlton Club. In the weary years of the Great Depression, with most of the neighborhood in the grip of financial hardship, it became a popular watering hole where scions of the Gilded Age came to drown their sorrows.

Later, from 1990 until 2001, the mansion served as a bed and breakfast, and then it was sold to a Floridian who announced his grand plans to renovate the building. Although the building needed some much overdue maintenance, it had survived largely intact with the exterior and interior in nearly original condition. The massive grand staircase to the upper floors, for example, demonstrated the high level of craftsmanship found throughout the home. The new owner's prospective neighbors were thrilled to hear that the new occupant would maintain the mansion's once grand visage and ensure its prominence in the neighborhood. However, this gladness soon turned into consternation and outrage when the new owner revealed his real plans for the residence.

On its Web site, the *Old Louisville Guide* describes the "progress" that then ensued at the mansion: "In the first few months, work on the interior included removal of a later wall dividing the original parlor. That was a good thing. After that, we can't find much nice to say about the work being done. The original heating system was one of the first things to go. Ornamental radiators began piling up and rusting in the back yard. Without heat, we don't need to tell you what happened to the plumbing over the following winter.

"The original kitchen and baths were all clad in marble, even marble showers. All those were torn out and gutted, the marble largely broken and unusable for later use. The original ornamental Victorian stove hood joined the pile out back to rust away. The back half of the second floor, and all but a great room on the third floor, were gutted and all the walls were removed. Even the third floor joists and rafters that served as ceiling and structural supports were removed. A significant amount of flooring was removed. Electrical wiring was dangling from ceilings for years."

Word soon reached anxious ears that every single room had been torn up, and none of the work completed.

The next stage of the debacle began when the owner sought a zoning variance to convert the building into condos. Even though current zoning regulations in Old Louisville have been written to prevent this type of re-adaptation, a fair amount of legal maneuvering resulted in permission to divide the mansion into a number of units. According to information from the Web site, "it could be seen that the master bedrooms on the front of the second floor had been gutted and re-framed into new rooms and even more of the historic fabric of the building was destroyed. Floor plans were altered and the original parlor was divided again, the ornamental ceiling removed and replaced by a common flat ceiling. The entry hall and grand staircase were divided and enclosed, but even then, much of the work was left incomplete." The building went into receivership in 2005 after the former owner declared bankruptcy.

An auctioneer sold off the building, renamed the Mansion on Third, as condominium parcels on Saturday, October 14, 2006. When someone snatched up the carriage house as a single unit, all hopes of the property going to a single buyer who might try to restore the property went out the window. A separate buyer ended up with all three remaining units, which will require an estimated $100,000 apiece to finish. For the time being, they remain empty, a sad reminder of the damage a single person can do to a historic structure.

Although nobody occupies the main house, neighbors have reported that some presence seems to inhabit the abandoned place. Lights have been seen flashing on and off in various rooms, and shadowy forms have been seen standing at the windows at times when no one reportedly had any right to be in the building. Could the old Armstrong place count as another of Old Louisville's haunted mansions? A commonly held assumption about hauntings involves the notion that construction projects sometime have the unintended side effect of awakening otherwise dormant spirits in a location. Once disturbed, these restless souls ramble about until a sense of familiarity reestablishes itself and allows them to recede back into the woodwork. Given the current state of the former Armstrong residence, it could be a while before these ghosts get some rest.

Chapter 8

THE WALNUT STREET BAPTIST CHURCH

Old Louisville is a neighborhood full of many picturesque views throughout the year. A glimpse of multihued stained glass sparkling in the late afternoon sun. A colorful bit of painted detail on a porch behind the delicate scrim of spindly branches covered in dogwood blossoms. A wintry blanket of white draped over a small front yard enclosed in the ornate curlicues of wrought iron fencing. Vistas like these come to mind when I think about the seasons in Old Louisville. But my favorite scenes occur in autumn when the threat of frost has mercilessly scared the green from the shade trees along the sidewalks and pedestrian courts.

Fleeting and pleasantly melancholic, fall weather predisposes one to the meditative side of things, and a simple walk can turn into an evocative stroll. One of the yearly views I take pleasure in emerges along Third Street in October. At the corner of St. Catherine Street looms an immense Gothic church, a veritable masterpiece of stone and mortar. When the towering maples that shield the three west-facing entryways put on their fall finery, it is a spectacular sight to behold. The yellow leaves, brilliant and golden, form a dazzling canopy for the rustic, wooden doors in their intricate lancet arches, and when offset by a cerulean sky, the ivory structure radiates grandeur and permanence. It is the Walnut Street Baptist Church, and its flock – one of the most active in

A strange winged creature has been seen hopping along the roof of this Victorian Gothic masterpiece, which was built around the turn of the last century.

the community – has a storied history in the state, making it a proud congregation in the midst of many proud residents.

Given the fierce sense of pride that Old Louisvillians feel about their hard-won style of living, it comes as little surprise that this hubris extends back to the early days of the neighborhood. The beginning of the 20th century in Louisville was a time of unbridled opulence that culminated an almost two-decade surge in residential construction and public architecture. During the heyday of the famous Southern Exposition, it seemed that new mansions sprang up practically overnight, and they dramatically altered the view along Third and Fourth avenues. These counted as two of the most popular thoroughfares for the city's elite – for those of established, old-money wealth and up-and-coming incomes alike. It was reported that in 1885 alone some 260 elegant homes went up in that area, signaling, as it were, the advent of prosperity and easy living for a growing upper-middle class.

Correspondents from national publications such as *Harper's Weekly* poured in and, notebooks in hand, they scoured the new neighborhood in search of stories and sketches to send back to their readers. Illustrations of spacious Louisville residences with solid construction and innovative design painted the city with a very complimentary brush, and word soon spread that a Kentucky city – in less than a century since its initial inception – had carved out an enviable slice of living for itself on the frontier. Local press ran with the accolades, and the Derby City soon became the standardbearer for the notion of the "house beautiful." In an end-of-the-year article that reflected on this incredible building boom, *The Louisville Times* of December 31, 1909, touted the local sentiment when it claimed that "nothing can rob Louisville of the distinction of being the real home center of the country."

As if to bolster this assertion, it added: "The stranger within our gates has ever remarked that Louisville homes far outclass those of other cities. Those who have enjoyed the privilege to enter many of them regard that privilege highly, and take good care that nothing may jeopardize it. Those who own them may realize the truth of these words, and those who do not, may doubt; but the Louisville home stands for itself regardless of the spoken or written word – it is the Louisville home."

In 1900, the readers of *The New York Times* got an idea of how

Tucked away behind the facade of the Christian Social Ministries building, only the top gable of the Gathright House is visible today. Ironically, the Walnut Street Baptist Church acquired the property that once belonged to the man who spearheaded efforts to boycott the church because of a scandal in 1900.

protective these homeowners actually were when a September article proclaimed: "TO BOYCOTT LOUISVILLE CHURCH: Fashionable Third Avenue Church Indignant at Baptist Congregation's Action!"

The Walnut Street Baptist Church, it reported, "the richest and largest congregation of the South," had recently sold its downtown location and had plans to build a magnificent $150,000 structure on "a fine lot on Third Avenue, the best resident street in Louisville." However, instead of adhering to the accepted property line of some thirty feet back from the thoroughfare, "the building line will be ignored and the edifice will go up from the sidewalk."

The article then went on to declare that "residents are greatly excited over the matter, but the church will not yield." When John Gathright, an adjacent property owner, confronted Dr. Eaton, the pastor of the church, with the allegation that disregarding the property line would devalue neighboring homes, the latter replied "that the church would buy the land when it got cheap." The article then concluded: "The church will be boycotted by the mansion owners."

The church demolished two homes on the site and went ahead with its plans to construct the grandest church on Millionaires Row. Today, the lovely front doors open right onto the sidewalk, silent and graceful reminders of the church's disregard for its Old Louisville neighbor. This might explain the unspoken animosity towards the beautiful Gothic structure on the corner of Third and St. Catherine that still exists in the neighborhood to this day.

Or else, it could have something to do with reports of a strange, winged creature that supposedly haunts the ornate towers and steep rooftops of Old Louisville's grandest house of worship. Described as half human and half demon, it has become known in local lore as the Demon Leaper. The many theories as to its origins only serve to muddy the waters of legend and ensure its position among the most bizarre stories the Bluegrass has to offer.

"My great-grandmother saw this vision several times when the church was under construction, and she always said it had the appearance of a large, bat-like creature. And she said it was jet black, too. That's how she always described it: like a huge, black human bat." Rose Hardy, a former resident of Louisville who now calls Brooklyn home, has repeated this eyewitness description of Old Louisville's Demon Leaper many times since she first heard it from the family matriarch many years ago. "When I was a young girl in the 30s, we lived on St. Catherine

Street in a row house that was torn down in the 60s," says the retired nurse. "It was my father's grandmother's house, and we lived with her for a time. It wasn't too far from the big church on the corner, and we had a good view of the towers from our room on the top floor."

Although Hardy never witnessed the creature for herself, a vivid image based on reports from others nonetheless remains in her memory. But given the many detailed accounts passed down by her great-grandmother, this is hardly surprising. "In my mind, this creature was always a frightening, gargoyle-type thing with dark wings and a hooked beak. That's how it was described to me. It terrified me as a kid," she recalls, "and I can still see it as an actual living thing, although, I must admit now, that it most likely never existed."

That doesn't mean, however, that Hardy discounts the alleged sightings of the strange creature witnessed by her great-grandmother. "I'm convinced she saw something, because she never came across as the flighty type to any of us, but maybe she exaggerated what she saw, or else, maybe she saw something that had a perfectly normal explanation. Maybe it was a big bird or something. I don't know. But I can still see those images in my head of a big, bat-like man hopping around the roof of the church."

Could a human gargoyle or Demon Leaper frequent the steep-pitched roofs of the Gilded Age structures in Old Louisville today? Hardy's reservations aside, tales of strange winged creatures in this part of the country go back to Native American legend, and early European settlers supposedly reported unnerving encounters with beings of a similar description as well. In addition, it seems that Louisville encounters with frightening flying oddities that began in the past have continued up to the present and seem to now focus on the Old Louisville neighborhood. There are also those who claim to have seen this creature face to face – recently.

Jonas Cartwright, a transplant from Florida who moved here several years ago, rents a third-floor apartment in a large 1880s house not more than two blocks from the Walnut Street Baptist Church. It was there that he had an unnerving nighttime encounter in 2005. "I have a little roof deck at the back of the house where I like to sit out when it gets hot in the summer. I was out there one night in August, my friend who was visiting having just gone home. I decided to enjoy another beer and then go inside and call it a night. I had to work early the next morning." Cartwright, in his late 20s, works in a local factory and usually has to be in for a shift at 7 a.m. "I had just put my empty beer bottle down on the table and was getting ready to stand up," he recalls, "when all of a sudden I heard this really strange whoosh sound, like a big bird coming in for a dive. Right then, a shadow came down out of nowhere and landed on the edge of the roof, just two or three yards away from me!"

Although the startled onlooker says the strange apparition lingered for just a fraction of a second before it bounded over to the neighboring rooftop in a single leap and then sprang into the air and vanished, he says the image that presented itself will haunt him. "I love ghosts and things like that, but this was something entirely different," he explains. "That sight will stay in my head till the day I die. It was something demonic, maybe a mutant or something, I don't know. But it was totally unnatural."

When pressed for a more detailed description of the creature, Cartwright says: "It was as tall as me, but completely black. It had wings that look webbed, like a bat's, and its legs were very powerful. When it landed in front of me, it kept the wings raised most of the time, so I didn't get a good look at its face, but it did seem to have sharp features from what I could tell. Maybe a pointed chin, something like that. I'm not sure, but it could have had a tail. I don't know." Cartwright also remembers one other detail that makes the chance encounter all the more chilling: "When the thing landed and then took off again, I could hear the scrape of claws or talons on the tarpaper of the roof."

Talons seem to be a common theme in descriptions of Old Louisville's Demon Leaper.

"I'll tell you straight off that I don't believe in ghosts and things like that," confesses Marc McConnell, another witness to the strange creature. "But I saw something in Old Louisville that defies explanation. It had big wings and claws, and it scared the life out of me!" At 52, McConnell currently practices law in eastern Kentucky, but he still recalls his days studying at the University of Louisville and the time he almost came face to face with the so-called Demon Leaper.

"I lived closer to campus, but it was a night I was staying over at my girlfriend's place. She had a gorgeous apartment in one of those huge mansions on Third Street, and her apartment took up half of the second story. She also had a little balcony that jutted out from her side of the house. It wasn't very big, but there was just enough room for two tiny lawn chairs out there."

On the night in question, McConnell claims to have seen a strange form on this very bedroom balcony. "It was pretty late, and my girlfriend was in the bathroom taking a shower. I had just come from the shower and was drying myself off as I walked over to the window that opened up onto the balcony. It was the only window in the bedroom, so I was just going to take a peak outside and see if anything was going on."

As with most of the residences in Old Louisville, there is usually not much to see when looking out a side window because the homes have been built so close together. "But even though you couldn't see that much, you could still look down and see the sidewalk that ran between the two houses. There was a very bright outdoor light, and you could look sideways and see what was going on out in the street."

As he approached the window, McConnell says he heard scratching overhead. "It sounded like something was up in the attic or maybe on the roof, and that's when something caught my attention on the balcony." A huge form had perched itself on the low railing of the balcony. "I hadn't actually gotten there yet and must have been just a foot or two away from the window when something swooped down and landed right outside the window. At first I thought it was just a big bird or something. But then I got a better look at it."

McConnell then saw something he can't classify to this day. "Even though there were some very flimsy lace curtains over the window, I got close enough where I could actually see through some of the larger holes in the pattern of the fabric, and whatever landed on the balcony was not a bird."

Fully illuminated in the bright exterior light, the creature then fell into a crouching position and folded in a pair of massive, prehistoric-looking wings. "I'd estimate the wingspan at seven or eight feet before he brought them down, and they were black, like the rest of his body, and he was all leathery. And it didn't look like there was hair or fur anywhere, just tough skin all over."

When asked how tall he figured the creature to be, McConnell says it must have stood about six feet when fully erect. "When I first saw it, my heart just skipped a beat, and my first reaction was that one of the gargoyles from the big church on the corner had come to life. But before I had any more time to study the thing, it jumped up into the air and was gone. As it jumped, I noticed that it had feet like a bird's. I could see curved talons as well." McConnell says that when he checked the railing the next morning, he could see scratchy imprints left on the mossy stone surface that were about twice the size of his hands.

Although I was highly doubtful when the first rumors of a strange flying creature in the Old Louisville neighborhood surfaced – it had all the trappings of an urban legend to me – I have to admit that the eyewitnesses interviewed came across as highly credible. In a worst-case scenario, I concluded, they had seen something perfectly explainable that had been misconstrued by the cloudy view of rushed judgment or else they had just imagined it. In any case, the strange reports sparked my curiosity.

Even though I normally shy away from the stories of cryptid creatures and UFO sightings, I decided to snoop around, just in case. I prefer to stick to stories of ghosts and hauntings myself because interesting historical connections often reveal themselves in subsequent research. But since sightings of the strange creature stretched back to the early days of the church, I hoped to uncover a substantiated correlation with the past in this case.

Not really expecting to find anything of significance when my research began, I'm happy to say an interesting story unfolded. The strange apples I discovered did not fall very far from the large and twisted tree of peculiar Louisville history. It seems that mysterious airborne objects and strange creatures have populated the skies over Louisville since the late 1800s.

Searching on the Internet, I came across an interesting article in the archives of *The New York Times* that proved invaluable in my efforts to track down sightings of Louisville's so-called Demon Leaper. Entitled "An Aerial Mystery," the piece was published on September 12, 1880. It described "a marvelous apparition" seen near Coney Island the previous week. "At the height of at least a thousand feet in the air a strange object was in the act of flying toward the New Jersey coast. It was apparently a man with bat's wings and improved frog's legs. The face of the man could be distinctly seen, and it wore a cruel and determined expression. The movements made by the object closely resembled those of a frog in the act of swimming with hind legs and flying with his front legs." The author astutely pointed out that "[o]f course, no respectable frog has ever been known to conduct himself in precisely that way, but were a frog to wear bat's wings, and to attempt to swim and fly at the same time, he would correctly imitate the conduct of the Coney Island monster. When we add that the monster waved his wings in answer to the whistle of a locomotive, and was of a deep black color, the alarming nature of the apparition can be imagined."

Although fascinating, the article appeared to deal exclusively with the East Coast. I was about to stop reading when another bit caught my eye: "About a month ago an object of precisely the same nature was seen in the air over St. Louis by a number of citizens who happened to be sober and who are believed to be trustworthy. A little later it was seen by various Kentucky persons as it flew across the State."

Could this be the same creature spotted in Louisville? With the exception of the "frog's legs," the description seemed very similar to those of recent eyewitnesses.

The article then went on to say: "In no instance has it been known to alight, and no one has seen it at a lower elevation of a thousand feet above the surface of the earth. It is without a doubt the most extraordinary and wonderful object that has ever been seen, and there should be no time lost in ascertaining its precise nature, habits, and probable mission."

But instead of attributing the mysterious aerial phenomenon to superstition or diabolical forces, the analytic mind responsible for the article opined that "either the flying man or some Scientific Person at present unknown has invented the bat's wings and frog's legs with which the flying man now sails through the air." And given the fact that the inventor of the flying equipment had not chosen to reveal himself, the author surmised that the flyer must therefore be "engaged in some undertaking which he cannot safely proclaim. In other words, he is an aerial criminal, a fact which explains the cruelty and determination visible on his countenance." Therefore, claimed the reporter, "the flying villain must have an object, and we have a right to assume that only a peculiarly nefarious object could induce a man to fly to St. Louis or New Jersey in hot weather and without an umbrella or mosquito net."

The author even went so far as to venture a guess as to the identity of the individual who had devised the flying get-up and for what purpose. His conclusion: It must have been the notorious American preacher Dr. Talmage, who "equipped himself with wings in order to study the interesting types of immorality from the lofty height of a thousand feet." And the best part of all: "He has flown over St. Louis and Kentucky – precisely the places which might be expected to yield a rich reward to an investigator of crime; and he is now flying to and fro over Coney Island, preparatory to preaching a scathing sermon on the wickedness and indecencies of our bathing resorts."

Intrigued by this bit of information, I made my way to the Louisville Free Public Library and began the arduous task of scrolling through archived volumes of old Louisville papers on microfilm. I figured if such a creature had trolled the skies over Kentucky, the state's largest paper would surely have mentioned it somewhere in the weeks preceding the September piece from *The New York Times*. Starting with the first weeks of September, I worked my way back, entertained by the many reports of local and national news, but increasingly disappointed as no reports of winged creatures surfaced. After two fruitless weeks I had made it to the beginning of the August issues of *The Courier-Journal* and was about to give up when an article caught my attention.

On August 6, 1880, *The Courier-Journal* had run a curious piece about "The Flying Machine." After scanning it, I realized that it followed up on a previous article and I traced it back to the original article, which had been written on Thursday morning, July 29. Tucked away back on page 5, it appeared in the "More Monkeying" section "With Other Edifying Morsels of News." The headline ran " A FLYING MACHINE – WHAT TWO LOUISVILLIANS SAW LAST EVENING," and the body told an unusual story:

Between 6 and 7 o'clock last evening while Messers. C. A. Youngman and Ben Flexner were standing at a side window of Haddart's drug store, at Second and Chestnut Streets, looking skyward, they discovered an object high up in the air, apparently immediately above the Ohio river bridge, which they at first thought was the wreck of a toy balloon. As it got nearer they observed that it had the appearance of a man surrounded by machinery, which he seemed to be working with his feet and hands. He worked his feet as though he was running a treadle, and his arms seemed to be swinging to and fro above his head, though the latter movement sometimes appeared to be executed with wings or fans. The gazers became considerably worked up by the apparition, and inspected it very closely. They could see the delicate outlines of machinery, but the object was too high up to make out its exact construction. At times it would seem to be descending, and then the man appeared to exert himself considerably, and ran the machine faster, when it would ascend and assume a horizontal position. It did not travel as fast as a paper balloon, and its course seemed to be entirely under the control of the aeronaut. At first it was traveling a southeastward direction, but when it reached a point just over the city, and it turned and went due south, until it had passed nearly over the city, when it tacked to the southwest, in which direction it was going when it passed out of sight in the twilight of the evening. The gentlemen who saw it are confident that it was a man navigating the air on a flying machine. His movements were regular and the machine was under the most perfect control. If he belonged to this mundane sphere he should have dropped his card as he passed over, to enlighten those who saw him, and that his friends, if he has any, might be informed of his whereabouts.

The August 6 piece that I initially discovered had corroborated a similar sighting reported by a D. F. Dempsey in the *Madisonville Times,* and an additional article on July 30 had described the hullabaloo created the day after the original sighting when throngs of visitors appeared at the drugstore to hear more about the strange flying object.

With this information in hand, I searched the Internet for reports of strange aerial activity or other anomalies in the skies of

Kentucky in the 19th century and was amazed to find a citation from the book *Weird America* that described a strange encounter around the time the Coney Island monster had been spotted:

"A tall and thin weirdo, agile as a monkey and with a long nose, pointed ears, and long fingers, appeared in this vicinity [Louisville] around July 28, 1880. He wore a sort of uniform, made of shiny fabric, and with a long cape and metallic helmet. On his chest under the cape was a large, bright light. His big thing seemed to be scaring people – particularly women – sometimes getting so familiar as to pull their clothing off. His favorite method of escape was by springing smoothly over high objects like haystacks or wagons, then vanishing on the other side."

Since this report varies somewhat from descriptions of Old Louisville's Demon Leaper, it appears that the Louisville area in the 1880s also harbored potential sightings of UFOs, alien visitors, flying human beings and/or any combination of the three. Because of the time frame, my first reaction compelled me to conclude that all these reports somehow centered on the same phenomenon. Ever the skeptic, I assumed that reports of whatever Louisvillians had spotted in the skies in August 1880, although apparently distinct from those of the Coney Island monster, must have been erroneously identified and misconstrued as the same thing seen flying toward the New Jersey coast. In any case, the probability of an unidentified flying machine, a strange uniformed prankster with superhuman abilities and an airborne bat-like creature all in the vicinity of Louisville – and all around the same time – seemed highly unlikely to me.

When I returned to the archived versions of Kentucky papers to find actual articles written about the leaping "weirdo, agile as a monkey" on or around July 28, 1880, I came up empty-handed. That's not to say the reports don't exist; it's just that I didn't find any mention of them. It's very easy to overlook documents when you're going through reels and reels of microfilm with tiny print, so there could still indeed be articles written about this strange creature that I just haven't uncovered yet.

Once again, I decided to return to the Internet to see if I could get any assistance in tracking down verification of the cape-wearing invader that had allegedly been spotted in Louisville. That's when I made some very interesting discoveries. It seems that the Louisville sightings tie into English folklore and reports of an odd apparition known for its terrorizing antics and inhuman jumping abilities. Known as Spring Heeled Jack, the miscreant first surfaced in the early 1800s and intimidated locals with its menacing, subhuman appearance and astonishing ability to elude capture with animal-like leaps and bounds. Many early versions of the unearthly being included descriptions of sharp talons, powerful legs and pointed facial features with bulging eyes that often glowed red. Most witnesses also claimed the odd being appeared to be cloaked in black, at times with something akin to bird-like appendages or wings. In those respects, Spring Heeled Jack seems to be a British ancestor of Kentucky's monster-like Demon Leaper. In other respects – namely the mention of intelligible spoken English and modified garb with mask, helmet and claw-like attachments on the hands – the descriptions suggest an entity of human design.

So, what, if anything, has been seen perched on the rooftop and steeples of the Walnut Street Baptist Church? An errant gargoyle brought to life by the chance encounter of imagination, light and shadow? A demonic aberration brought on by past misdeeds and neighborly disregard? An alien visitor intrigued by Gothic architecture? A costumed jokester hoping to liven up a dull evening? Readers can decide for themselves, but I like the notion of Spring Heeled Jack in Kentucky.

ABOUT SPRING HEELED JACK

Long before Jack the Ripper began terrorizing the dark lanes and back alleys of foggy London, a mysterious, menacing figure known as Spring Heeled Jack held Victorian England in the grip of hysteria. Although his antics never reached the level of gore and brutality associated with those of his infamous successor, this allegedly half-demon, half-human creature managed to frighten both villagers and city dwellers alike for more than four decades before he extended his appearance to other parts of the globe.

First documented in 1837, when a London businessman returning home for the evening reported an unsettling encounter with an out-landish being that leapt a high cemetery fence in a single bound, he was described as a muscular man of diabolic appearance with large, pointed ears and nose and bulging, glowing eyes. Later in that same year, his alleged encounters became more violent when he sexually assaulted a young servant girl and not too long thereafter caused a coachman to overturn his carriage and seriously injure himself. In both cases, witness-es commented on the being's devilish, high-pitched laughter and his apparent superhuman ability to leap great distances. As the press gradu-ally publicized details of the frightful accounts, the strange character came to be known as Spring Heeled Jack or the Terror of London.

Over the next several years the attacks escalated, and descrip-tions of the perpetrator grew to include a metallic helmet of sorts and cold, clammy hands with claw-like appendages. Some females experi-enced serious injuries during these occurrences, and some correspon-dents claimed that others had literally been scared to death or had been frightened into fits of madness. During separate incidents involving assaults on two teenage girls, reports claimed that the spectral being spewed forth flames as well. One victim alleged that "[h]is face was hideous; his eyes were like balls of fire. His hands had claws of some metallic substance, and he vomited blue and white flames." The other claimed that the monster had breathed fire into her face, causing her to experience violent spasms for several hours after.

In November 1845 the agile assailant became a murderer when he suddenly appeared in the dingy tenements of Jacob's Island and attacked a young prostitute named Maria Davis on a wooden bridge over an open sewer. After reportedly exhaling flames into the petrified girl's face, the mysterious attacker seized her in his taloned hands, lifted the victim above his head and hurled her to a certain death in the putrid waters below.

These incidents catapulted the crazed entity to local stardom when Spring Heeled Jack became the subject of several plays and penny dreadfuls, the serialized fiction publications in 19th-century Britain that cost one cent per installment. As the century came to a close, his appear-ances became less and less frequent, and the once loathsome figure expe-rienced somewhat of a transformation. Ironically enough, some eventually came to view him as a Robin Hood-type character as the memories of his early, albeit somewhat more depraved, antics faded.

In her online article "The Legend of Springheeled Jack" Sharon McGovern writes that "Spring Heeled Jack was seen leaping up and down the streets and rooftops of Liverpool in 1904, then disappeared from England for close to seventy years." She then goes on to say that "[b]y that time, however, he had become notorious in the U.S. Jack's American visits were first reported in Louisville, KY in July of 1880. There, he was described as tall, having pointed ears, long nose and fingers, and was clad in a cape, helmet, and shiny uniform. He accosted women, tore at their clothing, and emitted flames from a blue light on his chest."

Other sources report that from Louisville, Spring Heeled Jack then traveled on to terrorize other parts of Kentucky and the nation. On June 18, 1953, a figure bearing similiarities to previous descriptions of Spring Heeled Jack was allegedly sighted in a pecan tree in the yard of an apartment building in Houston, Texas. Three witnesses described a man in a black cape, skin-tight pants, quarter-length boots and dark, form-fitting clothing.

According to a wealth of information about the legend of Spring Heeled Jack provided by the online encyclopedia *Wikipedia*, his most recent appearance took place some twenty years ago. "In South Herefordshire, not far from the Welsh border, a travelling salesman named Marshall claimed . . . to have had an encounter with a Spring Heeled Jack–like entity in 1986. The man leaped in enormous, inhuman bounds, passed Marshall on the road, and slapped his cheek. He wore what the salesman described as a black ski-suit, and Marshall noted that he had an elongated chin."

Today, many theories abound as to the origins of this strange creature that supposedly crossed the pond and lurked in the streets of Gilded Age Louisville (and perhaps lurks here still). Some believe the being arose as a non-human entity of demonic beginnings, a bounding boogeyman, as it were, hell-bent on terrorizing the simple folk of England's secluded hamlets and backroads. Others, however, have argued that sightings dealt with a flying humanoid of extraterrestrial nature, an early Martian visitor to the Britain of the 1800s. But London writer Mike Dash, for many years a contributing editor to *Fortean Times*, has thoroughly researched the case of Spring Heeled Jack since 1982, and he thinks otherwise: "Jack should be classified not, as he generally is, with UFO occupant reports, but alongside other 'phantom attackers' and with reference to 'urban terrors' and other social panics."

In a well-researched paper that sheds light on the facts and fictions surrounding the legend of Spring Heeled Jack, Dash reveals that many of the initial reports dealing with the mysterious figure proved to be unfounded or had been exaggerated or misconstrued, something not altogether implausible given the less than enlightened nature of the subjects involved. "Nevertheless, most of the newspapers were prepared to concede that something must have caused the panic," he writes, "and several reported the rumor that a gang of noblemen was carrying out the attacks as part of a wager," a specially appointed investigatory committee contending that "the Spring-heeled Jack 'gang' was made up of 'rascals connected with high families, and that bets to the amount of £5,000 are at stake upon the success or failure of the abominable proceedings.'"

Although many more accounts and variations of subsequent attacks by the Spring Heeled Terror abound, as do possible explanations for their causes, a more practical allegation involves the notion that the original Spring Heeled Jack incidents might have arisen as nothing more than failed sexual assaults or misguided practical jokes that escalated into copy-cat pranks and eventually devolved to the stuff of urban legend. Given that 19th-century America often looked to Victorian London for the latest in news and fashions, there is little surprise that reports of a fleet-footed freak abroad could inspire frontier versions of the same phenomena.

Gilded Age ghost, alien visitor or nothing more than a practical jokester, Louisville's Demon Leaper has nevertheless joined the ranks of spectral beings that pepper the haunted past of America's largest Victorian neighborhood. The next time I pass the majestic façade of the Walnut Street Baptist Church in October, I'll make sure to look up at the roof and the towering spires in hopes of catching sight of the beast myself.

ABOUT OLD LOUISVILLE'S HOLIEST BLOCK

It seems that the unneighborly plans hatched by the Walnut Street Baptist Church to devaluate surrounding property values might have succeeded in the end. An examination of current property records indicates that the church owns many of the neighboring properties, including the mansion of the outspoken John T. Gathright himself. Around 1915, supposedly tired of squabbling with the large church on the corner, he vacated the property, and it eventually became the parsonage for Rev. Finley Gibson and his wife, Lucille. A subsequent anterior addition – stretching all the way to the sidewalk – completely altered the appearance of the mansion, obscuring all but the highest gable of the original façade in the process. The building serves as the congregation's social outreach center today, and the steady stream of downtrodden individuals in search of financial assistance carries on the church's legacy as a thorn in the side of its Third Street neighbors.

Oldlouisville.com is an excellent Web site with useful information about the history of the neighborhood, and visitors to its informative "block-by-block" pages can view an early photograph of the Gathright mansion. In addition, you can view individual pictures of many of the structures in Old Louisville and learn about their early inhabitants.

According to information provided, the 1100 block at one time counted as the "holiest" one in the city. "You could find the region's largest Baptist congregation at the Walnut Street Baptist Church, and living across the street from each other were the Roman Catholic Archbishop and the Episcopal Bishop of Kentucky. Even a Henry Pilcher, of the nationally regarded Pilcher Sons Organ Company, lived on the block for awhile." In addition, "the John N. Norton Memorial Infirmary was located on the block from 1885 until 1973, when it moved to its present downtown health campus location. The hospital was named in honor of the former associate rector of Christ Church Cathedral who was well known for his generosity and was called the 'Good Samaritan' and 'the pied-piper' by his congregation."

ABOUT THE NEUMAN HOUSE

One of the houses apparently owned by the Walnut Street Baptist Church today sits on the lot at 1123 South Third Street. My friend Silvia Zañartú pulled up the property deeds for me, and despite the many owners and endless legal restrictions, we were able to trace the documents back to the home's early days. Records suggest it was built sometime in the late 1880s or early 1890s, but the style of the architecture hints at a more likely construction date of the early 1890s. With its elegant flourishes and soaring gables, it has all the hallmarks of Chateauesque design, a building style that thrived in early-1890s Old Louisville.

Renowned architects Maury & Dodd designed the structure with cross-shaped windows and a stately façade with a delicate stone balustrade at the roof line and a graceful entry porch with airy, lacy arches. The Flemish-inspired dormers imbue the structure with a distinctly medieval feeling that make it a bit spooky at times. And spooky places oftentime harbor ghosts.

The specter reported at 1123 South Third Street takes the form of what viewers have described as a middle-aged man in a dark suit. "He looked like he was maybe 50 or so, and he had on a bowler hat. He was wearing a vest under his coat, too," says Arlene Douglas, a local factory worker who claims to have seen that very apparition in the fall of 1988. "I was walking home from church one Sunday night and just happened to be passing in front of that pretty old house with the stone front on the other side of the parking lot." The "pretty old house," 1123 South Third Street, had caught her eye several times before, and when she looked up, the woman "saw this old-fashioned kind of man on the front steps. He took a large watch on a chain out of his vest pocket, opened it and looked down at it. I didn't think much of it at the moment."

However, after a split second, Douglas says she was struck by the outdated clothing on the man. "I did a double-take and looked back, but he was gone. And it couldn't have been more than a second from when I had seen him. At first, I didn't think it was a ghost, but then, when he just disappeared like that, that's when it occurred to me that it had to be a ghost. He couldn't have gone anywhere."

The apparition of a man smoking a cigar has been seen on the front steps of this Old Louisville residence, a wonderful example of Chateauesque architecture.

At least two other individuals in the neighborhood have reported eerily similar encounters with an apparition at 1123 South Third Street that parallel Douglas' sighting, down to the gold pocket watch and bowler hat. However, no one has come up with an explanation for the purported specter. An examination of the early deeds show that

George A. Neuman, president of George A. Neuman Co. Drugs, occupied the dwelling from 1893 to 1918, but other than that, little is known about him. Although the names of subsequent inhabitants on the deeds suggest that many families occupied the home over the years, the passage of time has obscured their histories and family intrigues. When someone comes along and uncovers more of the mansion's past, some interesting tidbit might surface and offer an explanation for the alleged haunting. Until then, we'll have to wait and wonder.

Chapter 4

THE SAMUEL CULBERTSON MANSION

*W*hen people think of haunted mansions, they often conjure up pictures of gloomy, ornate Victorian structures that have seen better days. Usually in sad states of disrepair or sometimes abandoned altogether, the buildings are invariably populated with tormented, wailing souls or ghostly malcontents with a paranormal bone to pick. Sometimes their rooflines sport spooky, rickety turrets or towers with broken-out windows, and once in a while a rusty wrought iron fence will encircle a yard of dead crabgrass that looks like it came straight off a Hollywood movie set.

All in all, haunted places tend to connote images of negative, oftentimes ominous, spirits, depressing or malevolent wraiths condemned to a gloomy eternity surrounded by confusion and fear. And, in many people's minds, it's generally rare to find a place associated with benign entities and even more so to find a location with happy hauntings. But Old Louisville has a fortunate surplus of well-maintained homes, and every now and then a story surfaces about a blithe spirit in their midst.

One of these, a stunning example of Louisville architecture from the late Gilded Age, occupies the spacious lot at 1432 South Third Street. Few local mansions can beat its size – hardly surprising since the original blueprint called for more than 50 rooms. With its storied past, none can top the history and significance it represents for the community.

Known as the Samuel Culbertson Mansion, this beautiful structure figures prominently in both the city's literary and racing traditions, And some claim the rambling home harbors the specters of former residents who refuse to vacate the premises.

Ghost hunters Bobby and Patti Zoeller have enjoyed an overnight stay at the luxurious mansion, and although they didn't come face to face with the alleged haunts, they can recall an incident that left them slightly unnerved.

"We did have one rather strange event take place at the Culbertson Bed & Breakfast when we stayed there one night back in the winter of 2007," says Bobby. "My wife and I were the only guests in the old home at that time, and the owner let us roam around freely and explore the other rooms. We stayed in the Knights of Kentucky suite, which is described by the proprietor as the most luxurious suite in the city of Louisville."

Zoeller says: "I must admit, I cannot argue with that assessment." Over the years he and Patti have stayed at numerous hotels, including New York City's famed Waldorf-Astoria and the Plaza, but "the Culbertson Bed & Breakfast outclasses them all. Our room had a baby grand piano in it and a personal computer. That is where the story gets interesting."

According to Bobby, the couple had checked in during the late afternoon on a rainy Saturday, and, after looking around a bit, they went out to dinner at a local restaurant within walking distance of the Culbertson Mansion. "We came back around 9 o'clock or so and then settled in for the night. Everything seemed very nice indeed, and we decided to watch television for a bit before turning in," he says. "Earlier in the evening, while Patti played on the piano for a few minutes, I read my e-mail on the computer in the back room right off of the small kitchen."

Patti says the two slowly drifted off to sleep well before 1 a.m., both looking forward to the gourmet breakfast the next morning. "The next thing we knew, we suddenly found ourselves awakened around 2:30 a.m. when the computer in the adjoining room suddenly came to

One of a dozen comfortable bed and breakfast inns in the neighborhood, the Samuel Culbertson Mansion is a popular overnight stay for guests in search of local history - and ghosts.

life." The computer began its familiar hum, and the small room next to the kitchen lit up with the bright electronic glare of the computer screen, "as if someone had moved the mouse or typed on the keyboard."

Bobby says, "I looked over at Patti, and she looked over at me, and then we both looked over towards the computer and wondered what it could have been." The two of them cautiously got out of bed and walked over to the computer stand, "to see the thing all lit up and ready to go. What made it go on, we haven't a clue, other than to say we saw it for ourselves." Ten minutes later, the computer entered its sleep mode, and nothing else happened the rest of the night. "Needless to say, it took me longer than ten minutes to fall back asleep, and I think I was awake until around 4 a.m., waiting for it to come on again. But it never did," says Zoeller.

"Well, that's our story. Now whether or not it's something supernatural – I will leave that up to others to decide. We talked to the owner in the morning and described the previous night's event, but he didn't seem too concerned. We asked him about any other activity in the house, and he claimed to personally never have witnessed anything unusual. At least, that's what he told us that Sunday morning as we ate breakfast shortly before checking out."

There are those, however, who have had more convincing encounters with the paranormal at the Samuel Culbertson Mansion. It seems that the alleged hauntings center on the lavish suite where the Zoellers had spent the night.

"I didn't know the place was supposed to be haunted," says overnight guest John McIntyre of Cincinnati, "so when I heard laughter outside our door around midnight, I just assumed it was someone's children playing or something like that." McIntyre, a history buff and thirty-something attorney who specializes in immigration law, had come to the Derby City with his fiancée for a weekend getaway. "But when I realized it was midnight I thought to myself, who'd let their kids be running around at such a late hour? I got sort of mad, then, and got up to see what was going on."

Careful not to wake his fiancée, McIntyre tiptoed his way to the door and quietly turned the knob. "I could still hear the laughter outside in the hallway, so I was expecting to find someone out there, but when I opened the door and looked out, nobody was around. I stuck my head out and looked around, but the place was empty."

Scratching his head, he made his way back to the warmth of the bed, convinced that the invisible children must have run off right before he opened the door. "I was just about to crawl under the covers when I heard the laughter again. It sounded like two young boys running around playing. Immediately, I ran back to the door and yanked it open."

This time, however, McIntyre claims to have spotted the errant children before they escaped his sight. "I clearly saw what I knew had to be ghosts," he says. "Two young boys, maybe around nine, ten years of age. But even though they looked real to me, I could tell something wasn't quite right. They were all gray and white like in an old black-and-white movie. That's how I knew they had to be ghosts."

Before he knew it, the startled lawyer saw the spectral children vanish before his very eyes. "Just like that, they were gone. My fiancée had woken up by that point, so she asked me what was going on, and I just told her point blank that I had seen a ghost. She laughed and told me that I was dreaming, but I know I wasn't dreaming. I had been wide awake when I heard that noise."

During the rest of the night, nothing more occurred to interrupt McIntyre's rest in the lavish set of rooms. However, he does confess that sleep was hard to come by. "I never did get to sleep that night. I kept listening for that laughter out in the hall, but it was quiet the rest of the night."

The minor disturbance apparently failed to dampen the soon-to-be McIntyres' enthusiasm for the Samuel Culbertson. Six months later, they returned for a second weekend getaway in Old Louisville, John hopeful for another encounter with the juvenile apparitions. "I really enjoyed my stay there, so that was the main reason we went back," he explains. "But, I also wanted to see if anything strange would happen while we were there. The prospect didn't frighten me in the least; to the contrary, I was intrigued by the possibility."

Although he and his wife booked the same suite as before, their stay proved to be entirely uneventful as far as the supernatural. "I was sort of peeved nothing happened while we were there," says John McIntyre, "but I'm hoping to have another incident the next time we return."

Jan Arnold, an Oklahoma native who makes frequent business trips to Louisville, expresses the same sentiments. After a recent weekend at the Culbertson Mansion, she plans to return in the near future to the site of an unsettling encounter with the unexplained.

"Now if someone were to tell me this story, I'd probably think they were crazy, so I don't expect anyone to believe a word of what I'm saying. But I really saw a ghost during my last overnight at the Culbertson B&B." Arnold, an investment banker and divorced mother of three, doesn't strike most people as someone given to flights of fancy. And like so many individuals who report alleged encounters with the supernatural, the no-nonsense businesswoman claims specters would have never entered her belief system had she not experienced one for herself. "When you see something like that for yourself, it really makes you stop and think about things," she says. "It really changes your outlook on life, and then you have to start reassessing your entire beliefs. I suppose I always believed in some sort of afterlife, but when I saw what I saw in Old Louisville, it kind of reaffirmed that notion in my head."

It was a cold Thursday night in December when Arnold landed at the Louisville International Airport and claimed her luggage. As she guided her rental car off the highway onto the exit to St. Catherine Street, random Christmas lights sparkled from front porches and windows in the neighborhood. "I had never been to Old Louisville during the holidays before, so I was enjoying the change of scenery and the festive atmosphere." Nonetheless, Arnold admits that the bare, skeletal branches of the trees trembling in the wind did present a slightly spooky picture.

She parked in front of the Renaissance Revival structure that for many years was the most envied residence in all of the city and removed her suitcase from the trunk. Making her way up the front walk to the sweeping portico with its marble mosaic floor and twelve fluted Ionic columns of painted European red sandstone, Arnold had an unobstructed view of the stately façade.

Designed to faithfully reproduce the lines and colors of an Italian Renaissance palazzo in traditional Florentine style, the structure saw completion in 1897 at a reported cost of $25,000. The architect, the renowned Minneapolis architect William Channing Whitney, whose notable projects include the Minnesota governor's mansion, incorporated symmetrical features adorned with Renaissance motifs such as an ornamental arch with garlands on the second floor and a third-floor balcony to achieve a unified effect. One of the most remarkable, albeit hardly noticed, traits of the construction, can be seen in the glazed brickwork, which was usually reserved for fronts of homes in the Victorian era. In Whitney's design, this intricate detail continues along both sides of the house, hinting at both the cost and attention to crafts-manship involved.

"It's an impressive image," says Arnold, "but it doesn't even hint at the wonderful space inside. Every time I enter that house, I am amazed at the size and beauty." The architectural ornamentation fash-ioned on the exterior continues in the massive reception hall with its beamed ceilings, dining room and library. "The Louis XVI morning room and the drawing room remind you of a room in an English manor, and the dining room and library look like they could have come straight from a castle." With approximately 20,000 square feet of living space, the mansion's interior would have appeared indeed castle-like to the average resident of Louisville in the late 1800s.

"I checked into the Knights of Kentucky suite like usual and did a little work on my laptop while the TV glowed in the background," says Arnold, "Then I decided to turn in because I had a meeting early the next morning."

But not too long after the lights went out, Arnold says a strange feeling came over her. "It was like someone was watching me," she explains. "I'd turn the lights back on to check if anyone was there and I'd never find anyone, but I still kept getting the feeling that I wasn't in that room alone. Finally, I just convinced myself that I was imagining things and made myself try to sleep."

Peaceful slumber, however, would elude the jittery woman for much of the night. As she lay in bed and counted sheep to keep her thoughts from the uneasy sensation of being watched, Arnold detected the faint sound of laughter somewhere in the background. "At first I thought I was hearing the television from someone else's room, but then I realized that wasn't it. It sounded like real people – children – laugh-ing very close by. Little by little, it seemed to get closer and closer until I finally got the feeling that the sound was coming from inside of my room."

Throwing the covers back, Arnold rose from the canopied bed

and went to a nearby window. "I took a look outside to see if the sound could have been out there, but there was nothing. I was just about the pick up the phone on the desk and find out if they could do something about it, when something caught my attention."

She had seen a flash of white out of the corner of her eye and turned to see two vague forms race by her. "It looked like two little boys playing, one chasing the other, and they ran from one side of the room into the next room." When she followed them into the next room, Arnold claims they had vanished. "My first reaction was that two little boys had somehow managed to get inside my suite, and I was chasing after them to give them a good scolding. But that's when I had the sudden realization that they couldn't have been real."

When she thought back to the vision just seconds earlier, Arnold recalled that the clothing on the children didn't seem quite right. "They had on those old-fashioned outfits with big collars and sailor trim and they had the shorts, too. That's when it hit me that something wasn't right. Had I experienced a hallucination? I didn't know what to think."

Although Arnold concedes that she would normally have discounted any discussion of a possible paranormal explanation for the phenomena, she has been forced to reevaluate her values since the unsettling encounter at the Samuel Culbertson Mansion. "It's not like it was a terrifying experience or anything," she explains, "but it really made me stop and think. Having studied psychology some, I assumed that what I had experienced was a hypnagogic sensation, so I thought that was weird in and of itself. But when I learned about the history of the house later on, that's when I really started to think that I might have seen a real ghost."

Many skeptics of the supernatural have tried to explain away the phenomena of apparitions and hauntings with hypnagogia, the deeply relaxed state of consciousness individuals experience immediately prior to falling asleep. Long recognized as a source of creative thought and intuition, hypnagogic states – experts suggest – might induce in certain people vivid hallucinations that could be taken for ghosts, for lack of a better term. While others refer to them as waking dreams, the general consensus implies that would-be paranormal visions can occur as nothing more than imagination or mental trickery.

Although Jan Arnold has no problem accepting scientific explanations for the strange apparition at the Samuel Culbertson Mansion, one thing still bothers her. "I found out that there used to be two boys fitting the description of the ones I saw who lived in that house, and I wanted to know more."

This is where the house's interesting history comes into play, and as is so often the case, the past reveals itself in the paranormal experiences of the present.

The two boys Arnold refers to, William and Craig Culbertson, enjoyed many happy times in the mansion on Old Louisville's Millionaires Row, and it seems their memory lives on today in more ways than one. As the sons of Samuel Culbertson, the original owner of the lavish residence and one of the wealthiest men in the city, they enjoyed a pampered life that earned them the envy of other children in the area. This admiration spread around the globe in 1899 when a local author by the name of Annie Fellows Johnston published the second volume in a series that would garner her international fame. Set in and around today's Old Louisville area, the immensely popular books centered on the antics of a precocious little girl and those in her immediate circle, including her two best friends, William and Craig Culbertson. The second book, *Two Little Knights of Kentucky*, starred the Culbertson boys themselves, albeit remodeled as Keith and Malcolm, and it reportedly turned the youngsters into overnight celebrities. Buckets of fan mail poured in, and frequent parties held in their honor at the sumptuous family home gave outsiders a glimpse of life as enjoyed by the Kentucky aristocracy.

Today, the general public has largely forgotten the two little knights who roamed the halls of the impressive Third Street mansion, once upon a time captivating the imagination of a nation. Once in a while, however, viewers will get a glimpse of the original character that inspired the prolific series when they see the 1935 movie version with Shirley Temple in the title role as *The Little Colonel.*

Although Shirley Temple played the part in the Twentieth Century Fox box-office smash, the real-life figure went by the name Hattie Cochran. A little girl who lived in nearby Peewee Valley, Hattie inspired Johnston to write the original book in 1895 after the aspiring author spied the child walking along with her grandfather, a former colonel in the Confederate Army. Years later, the author recalled the encounter by writing "This morning a child of delicate flower-like beauty walked beside him. She was pushing a doll buggy in which rode a parrot that had lost some of its tail feathers, and at her heels trailed a Scotch-and-Skye terrier." But despite the innocent visage, the child had apparently learned to imitate the gruff mannerisms of the old man. "She's her grandfather all over again," remarked Johnston's cousin, "temper, lordly manners, imperious ways and all. I call her 'The Little Colonel.' There's a good title for you, Cousin Anne. Put her in a book."

This turned out to be a sage piece of advice, given that the original book grew into a semi-autobiographical opus of thirteen popular novels that would be translated into over forty languages. Johnston sold millions of copies, the Little Knights of Kentucky making frequent reappearances, and she became a very wealthy and respected woman.

This celebrity on the part of the Culbertson boys presaged good things yet to come to the residents of 1432 South Third Street. Their father, Samuel Alexander Culbertson, became the president of nearby Churchill Downs in 1928, serving as chairman of the board from 1937 through 1948. During these, the glory years of the Kentucky Derby, Culbertson often appeared in the limelight. Referred to as "the perennial cotillion leader," he entertained local dignitaries and racetrack guests from around the world. As a result, the Culbertsons became known throughout the region for the formal dinner affairs, spirited dances and trend-setting Derby parties put on in the lavish third-floor ballroom. During these events, envious passers-by often saw the family's theatrical tallyho carriage with a team of four high-stepping horses in front of the house as guests boarded for the racetrack.

In the early 1930s Samuel Culbertson achieved immortality in the annals of Kentucky Derby history when he commissioned the design for a festive "garland of roses" to honor the winner of the famed Run for the Roses. Culbertson stood proudly by in 1932 as officials draped it over Burgoo King, the first Derby champion to receive this accolade.

Samuel Culbertson lived on in the house till his death in 1948 at the age of 86, his longevity attributed to the fifteen blocks he faithfully walked daily to work at his downtown office. Although William died prematurely of pneumonia at the age of 47, coincidentally just days before the world premier of *The Little Colonel* on the silver screen in Louisville, his brother Craig lived to the ripe age of 83. Since both little knights of Kentucky lived on into adulthood, the question therefore arises as to how their child ghosts – if that's indeed what they are – should come to haunt the Samuel Culbertson Mansion.

This is where people's differing views on specters and hauntings come into play. Although reports of encounters with the paranormal undoubtedly stretch back beyond the beginning of written history, no one has been able to offer a broadly accepted explanation for the phenomenon of ghosts.

While some feel that hauntings arise as sheer products of invention or imagination, perhaps hysteria, others firmly believe that ghosts embody – in one form or another – the very physical energy that has transcended one life to the next. They can take the form of deceased souls in a distinct and separate realm who make periodic returns to the here and now, or they could be earthbound spirits inextricably tied to a corporeal locale due to an inordinate expenditure of sorrow, pain or misery. On the other hand, some scientific-minded theorists argue that ghosts occur as perfectly natural manifestations, consequences that can be explained away by the notion of time warps and the laws of quantum physics.

One related theory involves the interesting concept of place memory, which paranormal experts suggest might explain the apparitions at the Samuel Culbertson Mansion. Best described as a past event that has somehow imprinted itself on the environment, this type of haunt has also been called a residual haunting. Experts imply that images and sounds can be impressed upon a place and played back later on, similar to watching a film loop. This, in turn, could mean that no actual ghosts exist in these types of encounters. Rather, a simple psychic record of an individual remains from long ago, experienced when the conditions are right.

Given the large amount of solidly built mansions in Old Louisville, with their sturdy foundations and massive walls, it has been said they serve as veritable energy traps for past events that etch themselves indelibly on the fabric of their existence. Since the Culbertson boys led such pampered lives in the rambling family mansion, the consequent output of positive energy has been credited with imprinting their old stomping grounds with its own place memory, or a happy haunting, as it were. And those in the know of the supernatural workings of Old Louisville have suggested that, when circumstances coincide in just the right manner, William and Craig return to relive a few happy moments in the house, albeit only in the form of a residual haunting.

Place memory, hallucination, earthbound spirit or spectral vision, I cannot say what overnight guests in the Samuel Culbertson Mansion have experienced. Since it's very easy to reserve the inviting suite for your next stay in Old Louisville, you should check it out for yourself.

For more information about the Samuel Culbertson Mansion, call (502) 634-3100 or go online at www.culbertsonmansion.com.

ABOUT THE WILLIAM STEWART CULBERTSON MANSION

Before moving to Louisville, Samuel lived across the river with his wife Louise in a more modest mansion in New Albany, which the couple had received as a wedding present from his father in 1886. Ironically, William Culbertson opposed gambling in any form and had supposedly even disinherited one of his own sons for betting on the horses. Although young Samuel loved the races as well, he kept it a secret and waited until his father's death to move nearer the venue that would eventually earn him fame in Kentucky racing history.

As a child, Samuel Culbertson grew up next door to his New Albany mansion in an ostentatious residence in the Second French Empire style completed in 1867. The wealthiest man in Indiana, his father had employed architects William and Joseph Banes to complete its construction, which began at the height of the Civil War. With more than 20,000 square feet and 25 rooms, it cost almost $120,000.

Today, Indiana's Culbertson Mansion reflects the affluent beginnings of the Gilded Age. Hand-painted ceilings, gracefully carved rosewood staircase, marble fireplaces and crystal chandeliers only hint at the lavish lifestyle the family enjoyed while attended to by a staff of some 30 servants. Local millwork, soaring ceilings with gilt trim and inlaid hardwood floors round out the interior of the sumptuous house that Culbertson Sr. built as a wedding present to his second wife, Cornelia.

Storyteller Roberta Simpson Brown suggests that the residence of William Stewart Culbertson counts as one of the most haunted structures in the Louisville area. In fact, so many stories of hauntings abound, she claims, that since 1976, when the state of Indiana acquired the mansion, staff members are only allowed to tell the ghost stories for Halloween events. Nevertheless, it appears that the hauntings occur year round.

Numerous visitors and staff members have reported sightings of a female ghost in period attire making the rounds from room to room on the second and third floors of the house. "The general consensus is that the source of most of the paranormal activity is Cornelia, the second of William Culbertson's three wives, who died in her second-floor bedroom," Simpson says. "Her ghost seems to be concerned with the renovation and upkeep of her home."

Simpson herself has spent time in the lavish mansion, and her own experiences there have convinced her that a real presence lingers. "I have personally heard thumps in empty rooms, witnessed furniture that has been overturned in locked rooms, and felt the energy of a presence I couldn't see," she explains. "Some visitors have felt an invisible presence behind them, and some have been touched by unseen hands!"

In addition, inexplicable incidents have plagued various members of the staff. "Footsteps have been heard on floors when nobody was there," Simpson says, "and a heavy harp in the formal parlor keeps turning itself around, and a large spinning wheel has been seen rotating on its own."

According to Simpson, a parapsychologist associated with the University of Louisville visited the mansion in 1985 and conducted a thorough investigation. "He suggested that the house had a spirit of its own that might be causing the disturbances because it was unhappy with its condition." In addition, the staff supposedly received warnings about the strong negative energy sensed by the psychic on the third-floor around the "punishment room," a small cubicle enclosed in the attic where the strict Culbertsons reportedly locked their children when they misbehaved. Some have suggested this has bred no small amount of negative energy that could account for the hauntings as well.

Ghosts or no ghosts, the William Stewart Culbertson Mansion counts as one of the most beautiful historic residences on display in this part of the country and deserves a visit. They say October is a good month.

For more information about the William Stewart Culbertson Mansion, call (812) 944-9600 or go online at www.culbertsonmansion.com.

ABOUT THE STEWART CULBERTSON CARRIAGE HOUSE

History or Hoax?

Although many claim that New Albany's Culbertson Mansion counts as one of the most haunted abodes in the region, the carriage house behind the huge main residence enjoys a degree of notoriety in its own right for the ghostly events associated with its grisly past. In fact, the horrors that have transpired within rival any of those in Gilded Age Old Louisville for their level of ghastliness. That is, if they are true.

Aside from providing storage for the Culbertson's horse and buggy in the 1800s, the spacious structure also housed some of the family's many servants in the quarters above. According to information furnished courtesy of the *hauntedculbertson.org* Web site, in 1888 lightning struck the carriage house one autumn night and caused a terrible fire that destroyed most of the interior and killed every living being inside.

Afterwards, servants refused to occupy the carriage house because they believed the place to be haunted by the specters of those who had perished in the conflagration.

Allegedly cursed, the charred building remained empty until the 1930s, when John S. McDonald – who had purchased it for only $7,100 in 1899 – had it renovated for use as a rental property. Dr. Harold Webb, a respected doctor and dentist from out of state who had decided to relocate to a smaller town, leased the building and moved his family into the house in the spring of 1933. The restored carriage house served as both his home and office.

It seemed that normalcy had returned to the unfortunate structure. Dr. Webb soon attracted a faithful clientele, and his neighbors welcomed him and his family to the small river community with open arms. However, reports soon started to surface that dark forces were afoot in the unpretentious building that stood in the shadows of the opulent main house.

It started with disconcerting scratching noises from somewhere underneath the house. When the children started complaining about sounds of rattling chains and tortured screaming from below the floorboards, Dr. Webb and his wife, Elizabeth, dismissed the accounts. But when awful odors started wafting up through the floor, they started to take them more seriously. Eventually, they could not ignore the unending barrage of sounds and smells coming from the rooms downstairs. Soon the Webb children, locals heard, started telling frightening stories of a dark man who entered their rooms at night through the walls.

Although Dr. Webb supposedly investigated the lower level, he discovered no evidence of anything out of the ordinary and assured the family nothing was amiss. Nonetheless, the children's tales of the eerie nightly intruder persisted. And Mrs. Webb still complained about the horrible sounds and odors from below. Word spread among the more superstitious of New Albany's residents that malevolent spirits had begun to haunt the carriage house behind the Culbertson residence.

Concerned friends reported that the strange happenings were beginning to have an adverse effect on the physician's mental state. When patients started to disappear, the local authorities launched an investigation, much to the doctor's agitation. Rumors circulated, and

Webb lost most of his patients due to the bad reputation his erratic behavior earned him.

Then, on September 29, 1934, when one of doctor's remaining patients arrived for an appointment, he found the doors locked. Despite repeated knocking and subsequent calls, no one came to the door. After several days and no sign of the Webbs, concerned individuals called the police, who in turn received a warrant to investigate. They broke down the door and discovered a macabre sight.

The Webb family had been slaughtered, but officials could not locate Dr. Webb.

The remains of victims who had suffered unspeakable deaths littered each room of the house, but the most shocking of all lay beneath the living quarters. Police discovered a mysterious warren of rooms where Webb had conducted twisted, sadistic human experiments. Also discovered were a small cot and strange playthings in a small room, where the name "Timmy" had been scrawled on the wall in childish handwriting.

Sound like something straight from the mind of a Hollywood screenwriter? When an alleged ghost story seems almost too good to be true, that's usually the case. Even though there are those who swear by this macabre tale and claim to have historical documents to back up the allegations, a cursory search of most the archives of major newspapers in this country reveal absolutely no mention of the enigmatic Dr. Harold Webb. But his memory lives on nonetheless in the carriage house behind the imposing Culbertson home in New Albany – at least every year around Halloween when those in need of a good scare flock to the historic home.

Chapter 5

THE CAMPION HOUSE

The Samuel Culbertson Mansion is not the only home on Millionaires Row with ties to the area's rich racing past. The owners of Azra, the winner of the 1892 Kentucky Derby, resided in a beautiful chateau-inspired townhouse at 1366 South Third Street, and that address would later be home to Daniel E. O'Sullivan, the manager of Churchill Downs in the 1920s. The treasurer of Churchill Downs, Hamilton Applegate, lived in an imposing red-brick Richardsonian Romanesque structure at the former 1334 South Third Street. Applegate became majority owner of Old Rosebud, the winner of the 1914 Kentucky Derby and – according to *Blood-Horse* magazine – one of the top 100 U.S. thoroughbred champions for the 20th century. Anne and Alan Bird currently live in the large home, and they recently purchased the neighboring property at 1238 and have begun renovating it for use as a bed and breakfast. Known as the Campion House, the beige brick residence has its own connection to the neighborhood's equine past, but this connection is a ghostly one.

Given the home's history, it's not that surprising that there might be a ghost associated with the property. The reclusive former owner had boarded up most of the windows and doors, and the Birds acquired a home that had been sealed off from the rest of the world for decades. Old pieces of furniture and antiques decorated the musty

The playful spirits of two young girls in white have been seen on the staircase in the entry hall of this 1880s residence on Third Street. Are they the daughters of the original owner, sad victims of an early disease epidemic?

rooms, many of which must have looked much the same as they did around 1920 when his family, the Campions, bought the home and moved in. In some areas, walls had crumbled and decayed, but throughout the spacious mansion details such as delicate ceiling ornamentation and painted stained glass hinted at a lavish past.

The Birds have begun restoring the residence to its former grandeur so they can share it with overnight guests in America's most haunted neighborhood, but these projects require time. Although it might take another year or two to get the main house in shape, renovations on the spacious carriage house to the rear of the property have been completed and the Birds welcome company for overnight retreats at their cozy alley getaway. Although the accommodations ensure a comfortable stay, visitors might get a startle if they chance upon a ghostly apparition that allegedly haunts the alleyway in back of the main house. Guests need not worry, however, for it seems to be a benign spirit, that of a young stable hand who is unaware that years have passed since the last horse clip-clopped its way through the alleys of Old Louisville.

"I saw him," says Anne Bird of the boy specter, "one day out back, leaning against the carriage house." According to her and other eyewitnesses, the specter appears to be a lad in short pants with a light vest and dark cap. Hundreds of these youngsters would have been found throughout the neighborhood during Old Louisville's heyday when they were employed to run errands, do odd jobs, and attend to the horses stabled in the carriage houses. Although no documentation has been located to substantiate it, a neighborhood story claims that a young stable hand died in the alley behind the Campion House sometime in the 1880s.

"Supposedly, my great uncle died as a little boy in that alley running behind the 1200 block of Third," says Manfred Keppler, a resident of Sixth Street whose family has lived in the neighborhood since the late 1800s. "I don't know the exact details of it all, but we were all told as kids about my grandmother's elder brother who was killed one day when a team of horses got loose and trampled him. He was a stable boy for one of those homes on Third Street. I don't remember the date, but I know it happened when the world's fair [the Southern Exposition] was going on over in Central Park."

As if one ghost weren't enough on the grounds of the old Campion house, which neighborhood records suggest was built around 1884, there seem to be other specters afoot. Anne recently received a visit from relatives of the early inhabitants of her house, the Applegate residence, who claimed a former resident hung himself in the carriage house that almost butts up to the carriage house that belonged to the Campions. His specter has allegedly been spotted nearby on several occasions in a disheveled state of forlorn strangulation. Hanging tends to do that to a body, I suppose.

In addition two other ghosts supposedly haunt the dim interior of the main mansion, occasionally allowing fleeting glimpses of themselves from behind the handrail on the creaky staircase to the upper floors.

"I was coming from the back of the house to the front, to go up the stairs one night when something flashed in the corner of my eye," says Sherlissa Dawson, a former caretaker who spent many evenings in the old home with the elderly Mr. Campion. "So I looked up. And, all of a sudden, I saw a little girl crouched down behind the railing, looking at me. It scared the life out of me! She had her hands grabbing hold of the bars and just stared at me. I was scared at first, but then I saw she was giggling. Two seconds later, she was gone!"

Or so she thought. A little farther up the stairway, she noticed another apparition. Hands clutching spindles of the railing, a little girl with blonde hair stared down at her. "I thought the little girl had moved up a couple steps, but I was wrong. After a second or two, I saw that it was not the same little one. She looked different! But it was two different little girls, that's what I realized. This one had a grin on her face, too!"

According to Dawson, the sighting of the two apparitions signaled the advent of several months' worth of disembodied laughter in the foyer of the once grand mansion. "I kept hearing those little girls giggling all the time after that. Like they were playing on the steps or something. I thought I must have been going crazy, but then one night Mr. Bob looked at me and asked if I had heard the girls at all," she says. "When I told him I was hearing them all of the time he was not surprised in the least. When I told them I had even seen them once, he was not shocked, either. He told me they didn't show themselves very much, but I gathered from what he said that he had seen them himself. He did not seem to be too concerned, Mr. Bob. If he was okay with it, then so was I. I did not let it worry me very much. But I don't much trust ghosts, to tell you the truth. All dead, and stuff like that. Give me the creeps no matter how cute they are."

Although she claims to have seen the spectral children on the Campion House stairs on several other occasions, Dawson says the supernatural incidents gradually subsided and stopped all together. "It was like the more used to them I got, the less I would hear from them. Maybe they just got tired of playing with me and found someone else to joke around with. I didn't mind them going away, because to tell you the truth, it was a little creepy. But, it was just two little girls, so I suppose they were harmless. I always wondered why they were there, but I never found out."

When Alan and Anne Bird entered the Campion House for the first time, they hadn't heard about the spectral girls on the stairs, but they soon made an interesting discovery. As they assessed the condition of their new acquisition and made their way from room to room, a haunting find awaited them in the dining room of the Campion House. Hidden from view to the outside world for decades, a boarded-up window yielded a memento left behind by the original owner of the house. Iridescent and multi-hued, a beautiful stained glass panel hinted at the former life of the Campion House. Most startling of all, however, the delicately crafted image of two young girls stared out at the new owners of the Third Street mansion. Spirits trapped in glass, as it were, both of them had fair hair.

After some investigating, Alan and Anne discovered that the stained glass traced its origins back to the first occupant of the house, a Mr. Thomas Batman. The girls were his daughters, and the dedicated father had chosen to immortalize them in a stained-glass work of art that would survive as long as the house. Although they uncovered little else about the Batman family, the Birds heard that Mr. Batman resided in the house at a time when the neighborhood experienced tremendous growth and he took in local craftsmen employed to construct the mansions practically springing up overnight. In return, they helped Thomas Batman complete many of the interior finishing projects on the newly constructed mansion. According to the Birds, however, some of the smaller jobs apparently remain undone today, as is evidenced in random patches of coarse woodwork and incomplete detailing in parts of the home. For now, Anne and Alan Bird will just have to add these unfinished projects to their to-do list as they continue breathing new life into the old Campion House. Soon, it will be ready to lodge guests in the same Gilded Age comfort it offered in the past. If anyone spots the two little girls on the front stairs, I hope they get in touch with me.

For more information about the Campion House Bed & Breakfast, call (502) 635-1114 or visit www.campionhouse.com.

ABOUT CHURCHILL DOWNS

Although the history of horse racing in the Derby City goes back to 1783 when regular competitions took place downtown on Market Street, Louisville's most historic and famed shrine to racing was erected in 1875 at 700 Central Avenue. Churchill Downs, one of the most celebrated racetracks in the world, sits at the southern end of South Third Street, just a mile or so from the Gilded Age mansion of Millionaires Row. Once a bastion for the elite and privileged of Old Louisville, it attracts all classes of visitors from all parts of the globe today. With its history of dangerous thrills, lost fortunes and excitement, it comes as no surprise that rumors abound about ghostly entities haunting the fabled grounds of Churchill Downs. One of them appears to be a phantom rider, battered and bloody, who lurks in the twilight near the entrance to the clubhouse along Central Avenue.

"I was driving home from work in November. It was about 5:30, I think, and it was almost dark out," says Debbie Gifford, a middle-aged single mother of four who lives in a house several blocks from the track. "I was headed west on Central Avenue, and when I looked over to my left, I noticed someone walking along the side of the road, right next to the parking lot in front of the clubhouse. At first I just thought it was a child walking along, but when I got a little closer, I could see that it was not a child."

Gifford beheld the apparition of a jockey. But he was not walking; instead, he stood at the side of the road and stared at her. "He was almost transparent! 'Oh, my God,' I thought to myself, 'I'm seeing a ghost!' Then I noticed that it looked like his racing uniform was all dirty and bloody. I couldn't see up close, but that's what it looked like. I looked away for a sec, but when I looked back, he was gone."

In today's world, rife with urban legends and stories of hauntings, it seems that every city or town has at least one thoroughfare with its roadside ghost. Central Avenue is one of those in Louisville. The forlorn specter of a lone jockey reportedly began skulking around in front of the clubhouse at Churchill Downs sometime in the early 1900s and sightings continue to this day.

"My aunt always used to tell me there was a ghost from the track, but I never witnessed anything myself. I just heard the stories was all," explains Jerome Parker. At 35 years of age, the grade school teacher boasts that he has spent his entire life in the neighborhood around Churchill Downs. "When you live in the same place as long as I have, you get to know all the stories. There's a lot of history in this part of town, so there are naturally lots of ghost stories. I've heard them all, but the one you keep hearing about all the time is the Phantom Jockey. There was supposedly a rider who got killed on the track way back when, a hundred years ago or so, and his ghost is still attached to the place somehow."

Given the inherent dangers of thoroughbred racing, no one would be astonished to uncover a list of casualties associated with the racetrack. I located one particular story in *The New York Times* that made me think of the accounts of the phantom racer at Churchill Downs. Reported on October 4, 1906, the headline ran: "JOCKEY B. MILLER KILLED. Has Skull Crushed and Bites Tongue in Half at Louisville." Suffice it to say, the New York native sustained serious injury when several horses trampled him after he fell from his mount on Dresden. He died several hours after an ambulance removed his body to a nearby infirmary.

Why he chose not to haunt the hospital where he died, only the experts can say. Nor can anyone explain how his ghost came to haunt the street outside the clubhouse and not the track where he sustained his unfortunate injuries. But, then again, if you've been to Churchill Downs lately, you might understand why. The famed racetrack has experienced tremendous growth since its original inception as a Victorian pleasure ground, and massive side additions now dwarf the quaint clubhouse, all but obscuring the iconic twin spires. I'm sure that could throw any ghost off.

For more information about Churchill Downs, call (502) 636-4400 or go online at www.churchilldowns.com.

Chapter 6

THE CHARLES L. ROBINSON HOUSE

 South Third Street is another home in the neighborhood that has seen better days. Walk up the front to the immense brick mansion on the corner with Park Avenue, and the bank of some dozen or so mailboxes next to the door does little to conceal the fact that the former grand dame has been divided into apartments.

Many of the neighborhood's opulent residences met with this fate in the mid 20th century, when hefty income taxes and the financial hardships of the Great Depression made the upkeep of these huge dwellings impossible for all but the most affluent of Old Louisville residents. In addition, the government of the United States, in response to a nationwide housing shortage, paid property owners to rent out rooms or apartments in their homes to GIs returning from World War II. A quick glance at the city directories from the mid 1900s shows that in some areas of the neighborhood more than half of the structures had been converted into rooming houses or apartment buildings.

Today, the huge red-brick mansion at 1334 South Third sports a coat of pinkish maroon paint, with its intricate terra cotta details highlighted in creamy beige tones. The architecture has been described as somewhat eclectic, but an examination of the façade reveals clear Chateauesque influences with some traits of the Queen Anne style. The

Do strange pararnormal events in this chateau-style structure tie into a macabre chapter of Louisville's past?

bay on the left side of the façade features a massive gable with squat buttressing pillars at the roof level that balances an immense corner turret to the right. Decorative panels frame the middle-level windows, and ornamental columns support a second-floor balcony.

Despite the many apartments inside, visual reminders hint at the home's former grandeur. Intricate millwork features remain, as do specimens of beveled and ornamental stained glass. A grand fireplace with elegant marble details in one of the downstairs rooms suggests that the original Gilded Age inhabitants enjoyed a very comfortable life in the heart of Old Louisville's Millionaires Row.

Records indicate that construction on the home began sometime around 1892, and its first resident, Charles L. Robinson, lived there until 1913 or thereabouts. Since his profession was listed as that of a farmer and planter, the size and opulence of the original mansion suggest a very successful career. A Virginia P. Robinson lived on in the dwelling until 1921, and it appears that around that period the house started taking in other tenants as well. Mr. Robinson probably never imagined that his grand residence would eventually become home to many different individuals and families. Perhaps for this very reason, his ghost, unruly and dissatisfied, stomps around the old place in an apparent effort to disturb the building's current residents.

"I heard that he was an unhappy man, and that's why his ghost still hangs around," says Genevieve Hardy, a pre-med student at University of Louisville who has occupied a second-floor apartment for almost two years. "I don't know what made him so unhappy, but that's the story around here. And when I saw him, he didn't look too happy, either." According to Hardy, a cantankerous specter has paid her disconcerting nighttime visits on more than one occasion.

"The first time I saw him was on New Year's Eve, as I was getting ready to go out for the night. It was about 10 o'clock, and I was in my bedroom. Next to my bed I have this little dressing table and I was sitting there putting makeup on when I saw him. I had only been in the apartment for a month, so I had no idea about the stories associated with the house at that point."

That notwithstanding, Hardy claims she had experienced "odd sensations" in the apartment several times prior to the sighting. "I don't know how to describe it," she explains, "but I always got the feeling that there were people walking around in the apartment and that I always just missed catching a glimpse of them. It was like I could feel someone behind or around me, but when I'd turn around, nobody would be there. Like they had just run into the next room or something."

At first, Hardy chalked up the strange sensations to her new digs and the fact that it happened to be nighttime when she experienced them, but then she actually started to see things out of the corner of her eye. "One night I got a weird feeling like someone was sneaking up behind me and when I turned fast, I caught something out of the corner of my eye. It was like a shadow or a black streak. But I didn't think anything of it because I kept trying to explain it all away. The night I actually saw the apparition for the first time, that's when I realized it was all connected."

Sitting alone at the dressing table, Hardy claims an urge to turn her head seized her. "I just spun around on my stool and caught a bit of dark shadow to my left, but I got the shock when I turned around." There in the mirror, a dark form stood behind her startled reflection. "It had the definite shape and size of a person, but I couldn't make out too much in the way of details. I could see the shape of the head, and it looked like its arms were down to the side. I stared at it, thinking maybe it was an imperfection that those old mirrors can develop, but as I stared, I realized that it was coming closer to me."

With a shriek, Hardy stood up and turned to look. "I was positive I would see something, but there was absolutely nothing there." A glance back at the looking glass atop the dressing table confirmed that the black figure had vanished. "I sat down again and the mirror was back to normal. But then I had this fear that someone had broken into the apartment. I went and checked the other rooms, but I was all alone. It was such a strange feeling."

Several weeks later Hardy had another unsettling encounter with the specter. This time, however, she caught direct sight of it. "I was sitting on my sofa reading a magazine and I looked up, and there it was. The strange thing was that I didn't get the weird warning feeling I normally got. I just looked up out of the blue, and there he was. It had managed to sneak up on me without warning this time."

Hardy uses the word "intimidating" to describe the apparition. "I wasn't terrified by it, if I can say it that way, but it did seem to be very imposing. It was like it wanted me to know it was there and respect it, maybe? I don't think it meant me any harm, but I think it meant business." Staring at the figure, Hardy says the size and shape of it stood out. "Cleary, it was a man standing there, and he was tall. He had to be over six feet, I'd say. Even though the whole thing was like a dark shadow, I could make out some details. It looked like he had on a suit or something, and a wide-brimmed hat. I tried to get a look at its face for details, but then it faded away."

Most people would have run away screaming, but Hardy decided to get to know her specter.

Nonplussed, she sat for several moments and stared into empty space. "I kept telling myself to calm down and that I had just seen a real ghost, but it didn't make any sense to me. It was like my whole notion of reality had been turned upside down. I didn't even believe in ghosts, but I had just seen something that I could only describe as a ghost. I was utterly flabbergasted."

At that moment, movement on a nearby table caught her eye. "I had this little coffee table where I had all my school books and stuff, and I looked over there because one of my books was moving. It had opened up and the pages were fluttering like someone was looking for something in the book. It is hard to describe. Imagine what a book looks like when it's open on a table and the wind is blowing over it. That's what it looked like." With that, Hardy claims the book flew off the table and struck the wall several feet from her bed. "It scared me to death. I just sat there, frozen, for a minute or two, and then I went and picked up the book. It was my anatomy book." The rest of the evening, nothing else happened, says Hardy.

"But that's when I decided I had to tell someone about the stuff going on in my apartment. I was leery about telling any family member or friends, because they were like me – they didn't believe in that stuff. But then I remembered this girl I had gotten to know in an anthropology class the semester before. She was really into ghosts and stuff. We weren't friends, but when we'd run into each other, we'd talk and say we needed to get together and stuff like that. So I decided to give her a call."

The next day, the two met at a local coffee shop, and Hardy confided that she had "experienced a haunting" in her apartment. "I asked her what I should do. At first, she started talking about getting in ouija boards and having séances and stuff like that. But I told her I didn't feel comfortable doing that, so she suggested we get a friend of hers to come and check the place out. He was supposedly a big ghost-buster kind of guy, so I figured it couldn't hurt. She called him and we made plans to get together at my place in a couple of days."

When the meeting took place, Hardy says the would-be ghost-buster failed to impress her. "It turns out I knew him. He was a med student and we had taken a couple of classes together. I mean, he was nice enough and all, but he always seemed a little unhinged to me. He didn't strike me as someone who was credible," explains Hardy. "I couldn't buy his whole spiel. I guess I've always been skeptical of psychics and stuff anyway. He walked around the apartment and said he could sense a strong male presence there – but, duh. He knew that already. He had an electromagnetic field reader and said he was getting lots of signals, and he also said he was getting extreme temperature drops. It never felt cold to me, though."

When the psychic sleuth finally left an hour later, Hardy felt that she had gained little valuable insight into the unexplained phenomena in her apartment. "And when I went to study, it turns out that I couldn't find my anatomy book. I'm sorry to say it, but I thought he might have stolen it. Why? I don't know. But I couldn't find the book, and I know it was there when he arrived. In addition, far from helping me, I actually think that guy made things worse, because from that point forward the weird stuff happened a lot more," says Hardy. "Maybe he made the apparition mad?"

Whatever the reason for the increase in activity, Hardy still had a disconcerting presence to contend with. Within two weeks of the psychic's visit, she had tallied ten sightings of the dark apparition, and she couldn't deny the accompanying sense of unease. "I really started to get afraid – a little bit at least. It was like this spirit was getting more and more brazen with me. I'd get a weird feeling and look over my shoulder, and there it would be, sort of creeping up on me."

Hardy recalls one incident in particular that left her extremely shaken. "It was almost midnight and I had just returned from an evening out. It was really cold and I was putting my coat and scarf away when the door to the closet slammed shut right in my face as I approached it. And it didn't just go shut on its own. It was like someone forcefully slammed it. Like they were really angry." Hardy then decided it would be better to lay the coat and scarf across the back of the couch and quickly retired to her bedroom.

"I was going to make myself a cup of tea and watch a little television, like I normally do before I go to bed, but I decided I didn't need the tea all that badly. I crawled under the covers, grabbed the remote and turned on the little TV on the dresser at the foot of my bed." Hardy, however, wouldn't find the station she was looking for. When she pressed the power button, nothing happened and the screen remained black.

"Great. I figured the battery must have died, so I got out of bed to go and get one from the kitchen. And as I passed in front of the TV, it came on all of a sudden, full blast. I jumped back a bit and stared at it. I thought it must have been a delayed reaction kind of thing, so I went back to bed." But when she pulled the covers up around her and grabbed the remote control, the TV went off as suddenly as it had come on. "I pushed the on button, and nothing happened again. I tried it a couple more times, and nothing. I was really started to get frustrated, and then, all of a sudden, it flashed on and started blaring this awful noise at me. It was like high-pitched static."

Hardy raised her hands to cover her ears and was relieved when the television stopped its blaring several seconds later. Unfortunately, the only light in her room went off as well. "My heart stopped, and I just froze. It went totally black and totally silent. I didn't know what to do, that's how afraid I was. It seemed like minutes passed and then the light finally came back on, but it was probably only a second or two. In any event, I was happy when the room lit up."

This time the television set responded when she hit the power button on the remote control in her shaky hand. "At first, I thought that it was really an electrical problem and I tried to rationalize the whole thing. After all, nothing like that had happened before. It was always just strange feelings and apparitions, but when I thought about the slamming door a couple minutes earlier, that's when I came to the conclusion that they were probably all related."

According to Hardy, her heartbeat had just returned to normal when a dark shape materialized in the corner of the room. Tall and brooding, it seemed to be the same apparition that had shown itself before. "It was basically a tall, black shape of a man with a hat on, and he walked slowly from the corner on the right-hand side of the room to the corner on the left-hand side." As the form passed by the foot of the bed, Hardy says the form turned sideways and glanced at her. "I couldn't see the face, but it turned its head and shot a look in my direction. When he got to the other side of the room, he walked right through the door and disappeared."

Intrigued by the specter's gestures, Hardy got out of bed and walked over to the door where it had disappeared. Once again, most would have fainted dead away or screamed bloody murder, but not Hardy. "I was scared, I have to admit, but the way the thing looked at me, it was like he was trying to give me a message or something. It was like I was supposed to follow it, as crazy as that might sound." The door, she explains, opened to a small connecting room that led to an adjacent apartment. "I'm not sure what it was originally, but it looked like a small closet or dressing room. It was just a narrow hallway with some shelves and drawers built into the wall. The door into the other apartment was always locked, but mine was unlocked," says Hardy. "I guess, so tenants could use it as a closet. I used it to store some of my suitcases, though, because it was sort of rundown and dirty in there. I never would have put clothes or anything nice in there."

Not sure what to expect, Hardy opened the door and peered inside the tiny room. "It was dark in there all the time because there was no light fixture. I looked around, but I didn't find anything. Not that I expected to or anything." The doorknob in hand and ready to push the door to, Hardy then caught sight of something on one of the higher shelves. "It was something relatively small and flat. I realized at once that it was my missing anatomy book. I reached up and took it down, and sure enough, it was my book. I never go into that room, and there is no way that I put it in there and forgot about it. Someone put it in there, and I wasn't the person. And I'm the only one in the apartment, so how do you explain that?"

Something else had also caught Hardy's attention when she removed the book from the shelf. After putting the anatomy text with the rest of her books, she returned her attention to the shelf where the text had lain. "I noticed some scraps of paper or something up there and I wanted to get it down. I had cleaned out the whole thing when I moved in, and didn't want it up there. I got a rag and some cleaner and planned on dusting out the place. I don't know how I could have missed it."

When she ran the cloth over the dusty shelf and swept the paper scraps to the floor, Hardy beheld what turned out to be pieces of old newspaper. "It was like an old sheet of newspaper. Maybe they had put it down to line the shelf sometime long ago? But I don't know how I would have missed it when I cleaned the place. In any case, the paper was all old and crackly and broken apart in bits. In some spots it was totally black, but there were some parts I could read." An examination of the top line yielded an approximate date and the name of the newspaper. "I was only able to make out half the name, but it was an old *Courier-Journal*, and it was from Tuesday morning of 1800-something. I couldn't read the last two numbers, so I can't say with certainty, but it could have been 1880-something or 1890-something."

Intrigued by the age of the tattered scrap, Hardy took it over to the night table and examined it more closely under a brighter light. "Like I said, a lot of the print was barely legible. Most of the stuff I could read was very random – about politics and society basically – but one thing caught my attention. There was a little headline that said: "Scandalous Misdeeds!" And then were a couple of other lines that were totally black and unreadable, and then another little heading that you could only read the first line of."

When she leaned closer to better see the smaller print, Hardy read: "Body of Mr. Robinson victim of resurrectionists . . ." According to her, a large hole in the newsprint had obliterated the rest of the line and the subsequent article.

"I wish the rest of the article had been there. I wanted to see what it was all about," says Hardy. "At that point I didn't know that a Mr. Robinson had lived in the house, and I had no idea what a resurrectionist was. I just assumed it was some kind of religious cult or weird sect, but I knew that if someone was a victim of it, it had to be something bad." Several weeks later, Hardy discovered the true meaning of the word resurrectionist.

"I was in my anatomy class, and the professor started talking about something I had never heard about before, at least in this part of the country. She said that in the past medical schools and doctors were hard up for cadavers that they could learn from, so there was an entire underground industry to provide dead bodies for these people. Among other names, these body-snatching individuals were called grave robbers or resurrectionists. It totally freaked me out," says Hardy. "Because then that article I had discovered made a lot more sense. Maybe the man who used to live there had died and been buried, and someone had dug up his body to sell to doctors for medical experiments. Could that have been the reason he was haunting my place? That would explain the obsession with my anatomy book."

After her anatomy class that day, Hardy returned home with a plan. "Now, remember that I didn't know that Mr. Robinson had lived in the home at that point. But, anyway, I assumed there was some connection between the article and the haunting, so I decided to confront the spirit and let it know that everything would be all right." Alone in her apartment, Hardy lit a candle in her living room, said a quiet prayer to herself and reached for her Bible. "I don't read it as much as I should, but every once in a while I like to read from it. I picked out a couple of passages I found suitable for the occasion and read them out loud. Then I said a kind of prayer out loud and told whatever was in my apartment that I was sorry for whatever bad things it experienced to make it upset and asked it to leave and go on to a better place."

Either in affirmation of what she was doing or in repudiation thereof, Hardy almost expected the ghost to show itself during the impromptu ritual. "Nothing at all happened that night, but you know what? From then on, I never had a single problem in that apartment. Not so much as a bad feeling. After that, I became a firm believer in ghosts, and I'm convinced to this day that the article I found had something to do with the haunting. I bet someone who lived there had his body stolen after he died, and that explains the reason for the haunting."

Until someone locates and verifies the article Hardy claims to have found, or some other documentation that corroborates her story, her theory is hard to prove. When asked to produce the article about the grave robbers, Hardy says the brittle paper eventually disintegrated completely. "I held on to it for a week or two, but it just kept crumbling so much every time I looked at it that before long all that remained were pieces no bigger than a quarter. I just threw them all away one day."

Although the term resurrectionist might have been a new one for Hardy, students of the past know this word. Otherwise called grave robbers, tomb raiders or body snatchers, individuals who have broken into burial spots to steal valuables have probably been around as long as humans have been burying their dead. The practice of disinterring cadavers for doctors and scientists, however, became a phenomenon relatively recently and increased to problem levels during the 19th century with the proliferation of medical schools. The dissection of dead bodies had become an accepted way of teaching anatomy, and the acquisition of fresh cadavers, a subsequent and necessary evil.

Dr. Edward C. Halperin, dean of the School of Medicine at the University of Louisville, recently wrote about this practice in "A Glimpse of Our Past: The poor, the Black, and the marginalized as the source of cadavers in United States anatomical education," published in the respected journal *Clinical Anatomy*. When need for cadavers in this country exceeded the supply, he explains, slave bodies and thefts by grave robbers usually met this demand. Although the public knew full well that bodies regularly disappeared from their graves, the deterrence of body snatching required a great deal of time, money and effort. In addition, Halperin says that "the politically powerful tolerated this behavior except when it affected their own burial sites." As a result, the least economically and socially advantaged elements of society became the most vulnerable, and immigrants, the poor and African Americans became frequent targets of tomb raiders.

According to Halperin, "slave owners often sold the bodies of their deceased chattel to medical schools for anatomic dissection," giving rise to the terrifying stories of "night doctors" that became part of black folklore traditions. In conclusion, he points out that the medical education of white elites came at the expense of the marginalized in American society.

As it turns out, Louisville, with its thriving medical community and large number of poor, newly arrived immigrants and free and enslaved African Americans, proved to be fertile ground for these resurrection-men or resurrectionists in the 1800s. Old articles in local and national newspapers report that the gruesome techniques of the grave robbers received regular scrutiny up through the early 1900s. While most assumed that body snatching thrived in the colder months, when preservation proved less of a problem, an August 1871 piece in the *Louisville Commercial* showed that resurrectionists stayed busy all year long: "The stock of subjects is largely made up in Summer, and secured for the Winter by the simple process of packing in salt."

After an interview with a local grave robber, a reporter from the Louisville *Courier-Journal* shared the secrets of the resurrectionist trade with a correspondent from *The New York Times* in August 1878. The necessary implements included "a spade, a key-hole saw, and a piece of rope," and when done by a professional, the entire process took around eight minutes. They used the spade to remove the dirt from the upper half of the coffin, and the saw then came into play to open the casket. Once the upper torso of the victim had been exposed, the rope was lowered over the head and the body hoisted out. Body snatchers always returned clothing and valuables to the grave because authorities deemed the theft of those items a felony, whereas the theft of the body itself was only a misdemeanor.

The resurrectionist was then quoted as saying: "I remember once that the whole head of a woman whose neck we tied the rope around came off in our grasp. This doesn't occur often, and neither does the getting hold of a corpse like that last Winter with the small-pox, which, if you remember, spread among the whole class, and killed several students."

On January 10, 1885, *The New York Times* ran a sensational piece about "Morris Goldsticker, the young Hebrew who died suddenly in the City Hospital New Year's Day and whose body so mysteriously disappeared," who had "been found on the dissecting table in the Louisville University of Medicine . . . by private officers employed by prominent Hebrews." On February 26, 1890, another article in *The New York Times* described the midnight escapade in New Albany, Indiana, of "three prominent Louisville physicians, accompanied by two colored assistants, bent on a body-snatching raid in the interests of science." In this instance, an armed posse ambushed the party in the cemetery, "the result being that George Brown, one of the negroes, was instantly killed, and Drs. W. Edward Grant and J.T. Blackburn were captured, with William Mukes, the other negro, and they are now in the New-Albany Jail, while the fifth man, a well-known member of the Louisville medical fraternity, escaped and reached home in safety."

To show that the advent of the 20th century hadn't quelled the appetite for dead bodies, the headlines of *The New York Times* on October 26, 1902, screamed: "GHOULS TO BE PROSECUTED." The article detailed an astounding case in Indianapolis, where a grand jury had returned twenty-five indictments against various and sundry "ghouls" who had provided the Central College of Physicians and Surgeons with 100 bodies stolen in the vicinity in the previous year. The final paragraph of the piece disclosed the locations where authorities found some of the cadavers: "Ten bodies were found buried beneath a few inches of earth in the basement of one of the colleges, four bodies were found in sacks on the streets, where the hard-pressed ghouls had dropped them, one body was concealed for two days in a saloon, and thirty were found in cold storage in an ice cream factory at Louisville."

Could one of the many cadavers stolen during the gruesome heyday of Louisville's resurrectionists be the former physical shell of the spirit that haunts the Charles L. Robinson house? For the time being, Hardy's story joins the ranks of tantalizing speculations that form the bulk of the ghostly tales and spectral legends alive and well in America's spookiest neighborhood. In any case, it's likely to change how Louisvillians think the next time they're tempted to get ice cream.

ABOUT LOUISVILLE'S MOST INFAMOUS RESURRECTIONIST

Two of the world's most famous body snatchers, William Burke and William Hare, gained prominence in the 1820s when their theft of corpses for the Edinburgh medical community evolved into a shocking seventeen-victim murder spree, branding them two of Great Britain's most ghoulish serial killers. Although none of them achieved the level of notoriety and bloodthirstiness of Burke and Hare, well-known body

Simon Kracht, Kentucky's most famous grave robber roamed the cemeteries of the Derby City in the late 1800s. Photo courtesy of the T. Blackwell Family

snatchers proliferated in this country as well. One of them was Simon Kracht, an enduring and unlikely folk hero. Known as the "Resurrector of Louisville," Kracht was a German immigrant and former minister who was a young child when Burke and Hare committed their crimes. Sometime around 1863, he started working as a janitor at the University of Louisville's medical school and by the 1870s his unofficial job description had grown to include the duties of resident body snatcher. He was "the rock upon which our anatomical church was founded," wrote American Medical Association president and class of 1869 alum John Allan Wyeth in his autobiography, *With Sabre and Scalpel.*

Keven McQueen dedicates several pages to Simon Kracht in his entertaining collection of *Offbeat Kentuckians* and notes that "Kracht's side job was of such importance to the school that his likeness was included in an album of 44 photographs featuring the medical faculty." An accompanying albumen print photo shows Kracht posing with a spade in his right hand and a gunnysack with protruding skull draped dramatically over his shoulders. As McQueen reports, the *Louisville Ledger* described him as someone "Dickens could have written an entire new book about. In his makeup he was the very man to adorn the novelist's page – low, puffy, blear-eyed, peculiar. He was never known to wear a coat, whatever might be the range of the mercury, and his upper person was only protected from the vulgar gaze of humanity by a thick woolen shirt of a leaden hue, which he wore in both winter and summer."

Despite his gruesome demeanor, says McQueen, "Kracht was immensely popular with both the faculty and the medical students, who called him 'Old Simon.' The students were aware that his contributions made their education possible. Possibly they were relieved someone else was willing to do the dirty work." Part of the dirty work, incidentally, included the disposal of post-dissection remains, which Kracht usually tossed down a very deep, dry well at the corner of Eighth and Chestnut Streets in downtown Louisville.

"But," as McQueen points out, "the life of a resurrectionist isn't all fun and pleasure." Karma caught up to Kracht one day. After several years of domestic discord, financial adversity and familial intrigue, that day came on November 12, 1875. After a bitter argument with his wife in their quarters at the university, the despondent Kracht emerged and helped himself to a lethal dose of morphine. By the time his wife found him and secured first aid, however, fate had already run its course. At the age of 53, the Resurrector of Louisville lay dead.

Most likely as a sign of their esteem for Old Simon, the administration of the Medical School hosted his well-attended funeral at the medical building two days later. The *Courier-Journal* ran an obituary the next day that read: "In his humble way Simon was a faithful servant of medical science, and the tribute of respect and appreciation which was paid his remains yesterday was eminently appropriate. It will be difficult for the faculty to find one who can fill his place."

Kracht lies interred at Cave Hill Cemetery, and the firm, fully rounded mound of dirt over the grave suggests that his successors failed to plunder it and return their role model to the dissection table. Nonetheless, rumors abound that the medical school, the location of so many anatomy lessons at the expense of countless tombless victims, harbors a disheveled specter today. People usually report seeing a canvas sack slung over its shoulder. But, I'll leave those accounts for another book.

Chapter 7

THE CHARLES P. ROBINSON HOUSE

*I*n most neighborhoods, you'd be hard pressed to find two haunted houses on the same street, let alone two with former residents of the same name. Just a little more than a block down and across the street from 1334 South Third Street sits another mansion that was home to another Charles Robinson: Charles P. Robinson. A solid brick dwelling built around 1906, the structure at 1407 South Third Street has three floors and shows traits of the Italian Revival style. An examination of the 1910 *Caron's City Directory* reveals that Robinson worked as president of Robinson Bros. & Co., a prestigious hardware business located in the city center.

Michael Bennet, an amateur historian who majored in English at the University of Louisville, lived in one of the home's apartments for more than three years. Although the self-proclaimed skeptic has no belief in the afterlife, his experiences in the Third Street apartment have led him to a re-examination of the world in which he lives. He still doubts the possibility of life after death, but he has become a firm believer in the unexplained. "I guess we as human beings don't know it all because there are just too many things in this world that we do not understand," he says. "And there are many things that the experts have not been able to explain. I've witnessed some things that defy a logical explanation, so that's why I can say this with confidence. In the time I've been here, I've come to believe that Old Louisville is a place that is full of unexplained occurrences."

Although his current Old Louisville residence has yet to provide him with any paranormal experiences, Bennet now believes that he witnessed unexplained phenomena in both of his previous apartments. "After what happened to me in the Third Street apartment, I started thinking that maybe some of the little creaks and groans I had been hearing in my apartments before could have been something paranormal. And by 'paranormal' I mean something 'outside the normal.' It doesn't have to mean ghosts and stuff like that."

When Bennet took up residence in the building at 1407 South Third Street, he had no idea that the apartment came with its own variety of paranormal occurrences. "At first, there were noises, apparently groans and footsteps, but I just assumed it came from the neighbors," he says. "I didn't think anything of it. And because I love history so much, as soon as I moved in I tried doing some research on the house to see who used to live here. Even though I didn't find out very much, I managed to talk to some people in the neighborhood who said the place was haunted. They said that it was because the man who built it suffered a lot."

When asked what type of suffering had been endured in the house, the Chicago native says his informants could only tell him that it stemmed from sorrow dealing with the man's wife. "Other than that, they didn't know any details. I guess it was like part of a legend in the area, and that's all that remained – the fact that it had something to do with his wife." Aside from some general data about the construction date of the home and professional information about its first occupant, Bennet turned up no additional information about the past lives of 1407 South Third Street.

While Bennet had uncovered stories about a ghost on the premises, he didn't expect to add his own first-hand experience to the repertoire one day. "Like I said, at first, when I heard all the stomping around and such, I thought it was coming from one of the neighboring units, but then something happened that convinced me otherwise."

Bennet had been hearing sounds for a while before his first encounter. But he returned home after a day of classes at the university, and after fixing himself a sandwich in the kitchen, he walked into the living room and turned on the television. "I was just getting ready to plop myself down in the easy chair in front of the TV when I noticed footsteps coming up the stairs. Since my apartment is right off the stairs, I didn't think too much of it, though. I sat down and started to eat my sandwich."

Within several minutes, Bennet started to wonder about the loud steps outside. "They just wouldn't stop. Up and down, up and down. They kept on going. That's when I figured someone was moving in or out of one of the apartments above me. So I decided to get up and see what was going on." However, before he could raise himself out of the chair, the door to his apartment flew open. "The door that leads out to the stairs just opened up, and it sounded like someone walked right into my place. I heard several loud steps, that door slammed shut, and then came several more loud steps across the hallway. But, then, what really shocked me was how the door to my bedroom flew open and then slammed shut. Just like someone walked in from the landing and then through two separate doors, closing each one as they passed through."

After the second door closed with a slam, Bennet says several more distinct footsteps faded away into silence. "What do you do when something like that happens?" he asks. "It was clear that something had just opened the door to my apartment, entered and then walked into my bedroom. I didn't see anything except the doors opening on their own, but I knew there was something inside with me."

He hesitated for several moments, and then got up the courage to walk over and open the door to his bedroom. "I don't know what I expected to find," explains Bennet, "but I was convinced that something had gone into my room. Whether or not I would actually see it was another thing, but something had gone into my room. And I'm not ashamed to say it, but my hands were shaking as I reached for the knob."

Bennet cautiously pushed the door ajar and slowly opened it all the way. But much to his chagrin and little to his surprise, the room was devoid of any visible source of the spectral footsteps he had just experienced. "It was totally empty. I almost expected someone or something to jump out at me, but nobody was there. I poked my head in the closet and looked around for a bit, but then I gave up and went back to the living room."

Although he thought the incident over, another surprise awaited Bennet once he sat back down in his chair. "All I wanted to do was
eat my sandwich and watch a little TV," he says, "and I wasn't in the
mood for ghosts and things. Not like I even believe in ghosts or anything, but I knew something weird had just happened, and I figured
that that was it." But that wasn't it for Bennet.

"I had just settled back in the chair and was about to take a bite
of my sandwich when it happened all over again! But this time, in
reverse. I heard several loud steps, the door to the bedroom flew open
and then slammed shut, and then I heard more steps and the door to the
stairs outside flew open and slammed shut." Bennet then heard loud
steps making their way down the stairs. "This time I shot right up and
out of the chair and ran to the door. I tried to yank it open, but that's
when I remembered that the door had been dead bolted. I unlocked it
and looked out into the stairwell, but once again, there was nothing
there."

"That's when I really got spooked," he says. "The hair just stood
straight up on the back of my neck and arms, and I just got this really
eerie feeling. It was like I knew the place was haunted for a fact, because
that had to be the only explanation, and that's what caused the sensation. It was really quiet, too; so quiet you could hear a pin drop. It was
wild. I just looked around and waited for something to show itself, but
nothing ever appeared."

At least, nothing appeared that afternoon. Several weeks later,
Bennet got his first glimpse of the entity that appeared to be haunting
his digs. "I was sort of getting used to the doors opening and closing,"
he explains, "because it would happen every couple of days or so. Still,
it really did give me the creeps. But after the first few times, I got the
sense that whatever was doing the slamming wasn't out to hurt me or
anything. I realized it was part of the house and came to accept it. I did-
n't think that I'd actually see the ghost or whatever it was in person one
day."

But several days after an exceptionally active night of slamming
doors and loud footsteps, a shadowy form surprised Bennet as he walked
out of his bedroom. "I was headed into the kitchen to make a pot of cof-

fee and I just froze as I passed through the doorway into the common room that joins the kitchen and living room with my room. And I saw this thing standing there. I don't know how else to describe it. It was a shape that was sort of human in form. You couldn't really see any details, but it seemed that it was like a blurry person standing there, if that makes even the tiniest bit of sense."

Although Bennet says the apparition displayed no identifiable human traits, other than its general shape, he nonetheless had the distinct impression that a male entity stood before him. "I don't know if it was the size or what, but I'm pretty sure it was a man. I don't know what he wanted, but it seemed that the air around me got very heavy and oppressive. I started to feel overcome with emotion, too. Like I was really sad about something. The figure finally went away a couple of seconds after that, but I still felt sad for days afterwards. Like I was infected with depression or something."

A week later, Bennet claims to have experienced something similar in the very same spot and at the same time of day. "It was going on 4 o'clock, I believe, and I was leaving my bedroom again, but I didn't actually see anything that time. Instead, I got that same feeling I had before. The air got thick with electricity and sadness. I couldn't see anything, but I could feel that someone was there with me. Then, it just sort of went away. But I still felt sad afterwards." As with his previous encounter, Bennet says a sense of depression lingered with him for days after.

The strange entity never showed itself again, but Bennet claims that periodic incidents with the slamming doors and unexplained footfalls plagued him during the remainder of his tenancy at 1407 South Third Street. "I got so I could deal with the footsteps and all that," he explains, "but I don't think I could have dealt with that weird manifestation for very long. It seemed like it always drained the energy away from me. I would have been a basket case."

Cary Plainfield, a parapsychological expert from Bakersfield, California, suggests this feeling of emotional drainage accurately sums up what in fact transpires when an apparition chooses to manifest itself. "Spirits can draw on nearby energy sources for their power," he explains, "and while this could mean that they drain batteries of their power or cause electrical devices to flicker on and off, they often tap into an individual's psychic energy and use it to show themselves."

Plainfield and Bennet met several years ago at a monthly meeting of one of the Louisville-area paranormal groups. Bennet had decided to attend the meeting to see if he could learn something about the strange occurrences he had experienced in his apartment; Plainfield, who was in town assisting in "a case of exorcism involving the Vatican," says he went to meet other aficionados of the supernatural in the Louisville area. As chance would have it, the two met and Bennet shared his accounts with Plainfield.

"I travel around the country quite a bit," he says. "I like to find out what is going on – paranormally speaking – in whichever region I happen to find myself. If I have the time, I am more than willing to lend my services when they are in need." Because of this, he agreed to pay Bennet a visit in his Third Street apartment. "I have clairvoyant abilities," says Plainfield, "and I am often in a position to communicate with persons who have crossed over to the other side. This comes in handy when a true case of haunting is involved. And by 'true haunting' I mean a situation where a spirit from the other side has become tethered to a certain physical location."

According to Bennet, Plainfield arrived at the Third Street apartment on a Thursday evening, just hours before he was to catch a flight back to California. "The place had been pretty quiet, no slamming doors or anything for almost a week," recalls Bennet, "but I was still hoping that something would happen while Cary was there. I had never really used a medium in this kind of situation, so I was a bit anxious about the outcome." Plainfield entered the apartment and claims that "a sense of deep sadness enveloped" him.

"I knew there was a tragedy involved somehow, I knew that right away," he says. "Whenever you get that oppressive feeling when you walk into a space, that's a good indicator that something bad happened. It's like there's a very heavy weight on your chest. It usually means that someone died a sudden death on the spot. We're talking suicide or murder in most cases."

As Plainfield moved from room to room in the apartment, the mood of oppression followed him. "Usually it's most prevalent in a certain area, like a victim's bedroom or some other area where the individual spent a lot of time, but I got that sad feeling wherever I roamed in the apartment. It didn't subside from one room to the next; for that reason I suspect that the pervasive feeling would have accompanied me had I managed to get into other parts of the old house." After half an hour of reading the apartment, Plainfield came to the conclusion that a male presence still lingered in the old mansion. "But I have to admit that I got a very garbled message," he explains. "Although a male entity made itself known to me, I was picking up on a very strong female presence as well."

Many are skeptical of self-proclaimed mediums and psychics and tend to take whatever they say with a grain of salt. Having been on various investigations myself, and seeing them in action, I have come across too many who are, in my opinion, charlatans. That's not to say that some haven't impressed me with readings that seemed to corroborate information known only to me or that would later be verified. If they can provide some information that backs up a particular claim to a haunting, that's great. But I usually don't expect anything when a psychic is involved.

This was the case with Cary Plainfield as well. Although I had no reason to believe that he was inventing things, there's nothing to say he couldn't have expounded on the information already conveyed by Bennet. That's one of the things I've noticed about mediums: They tend to regurgitate a lot of the details already surrendered to them by unwitting informants. For this reason, I determined to listen to Plainfield's account with objectivity and skepticism.

After hearing his impressions of the purported haunting in the old Robinson mansion, I remained unimpressed. Since Bennet's initial reports had excited my curiosity I decided to add his story to my list of places to be researched. Several months later, I followed up with Bennet. According to him, the loud footsteps and door slamming had reoccurred on a regular basis, several times to such an extent that the noise bothered his neighbors. But none of the footsteps ever materialized when I was present.

He also invited several members of an Ohio-based paranormal group to conduct an investigation in his apartment, and they "experienced several sudden and drastic drops in temperature and some extremely high electromagnetic field readings." A psychic in the group had picked up on "a dominant male presence" as well. Like Plainfield, the California clairvoyant, this medium also mentioned some strong connection to a female. "The psychic lady told me that the woman she had sensed was somehow the source of the man's suffering. Almost like he was tormented by her."

I found it interesting that two sources – each supposedly independent of the other –brought up this male-female connection, so I set out to see if I could unearth any evidence to substantiate these claims. With little to go on save the approximate year the house had been built and the name of its first occupants, I started working my way through microfiched versions of old Louisville newspapers from the early 1900s.

After two weeks I discovered in the society pages one mention of "Mr. Charles Robinson, the respected gentleman of Third Avenue" and not much else – other than the fact that Robinson counted as a rather common name in Louisville back then.

Undaunted, I turned to the online versions of newspaper archives across the country and began searching for the name of Charles Robinson from that approximate era. I uncovered several from around the country, but none with a Louisville connection. Then, bearing in mind that the psychic had mentioned an unknown tragedy relevant to the case, I started doing searches involving "Louisville" and "death" or "murder" or "accident."

As it turns out, Louisville enjoyed a reputation as an extremely rough-and-tumble kind of town, in an equally rough-and-tumble kind of state. Frequent shootings, stabbings, throat-slittings, robberies and beatings in Louisville peppered newspapers from coast to coast. When no instances of violence involving the Robinson name surfaced, I started using other key words such as "tragedy," "assassination," and finally "suicide."

That yielded nothing as well, so I just searched the words "Charles Robinson" and "Louisville." That's when I found an interesting article archived in *The New York Times* online database. Although two things didn't add up in my mind, it did present a story about an incident in New York City that offers a potential explanation for the haunting at 1407 South Third Street.

The article ran on October 10, 1887 – some years before Robinson moved into his comfortable residence on Millionaires Row – and the headline read: "LEAPED FROM A WINDOW. A Hysterical Woman Kills Herself on Madison Avenue." The first sentence explained that "Mrs. Ella Robinson, the wife of Charles Robinson, a wholesale hardware merchant of Louisville, jumped from a third-story window at 106 Madison-avenue yesterday after-noon and sustained injuries from which she died a few hours later." The article described the unfortunate mother of three as a comely thirty-year-old woman with a good figure, dark complexion and hazel eyes, "showing all the evidence of refinement," who had been sent to New York for treatment of a nervous condition.

After detailing the arrangements for her medical care, the reporter described a tormented soul who was "hysterical nearly all the time until Saturday evening, when she became quiet." She attended services at a nearby church the next day, returned to her room at a boarding house and removed her outer garments before lying down to rest. Tragedy struck around 3:30 that afternoon after the nurse gave the woman a glass of milk and stepped into the next room to put away the pitcher: When she returned "Mrs. Robinson was not in the room. The nurse ran to the window, and saw the mangled form of her patient lying in the area below." Her physician was summoned, and when he examined the woman, he discovered she had fractured her skull and suffered three broken ribs. "She died at 7:30 o'clock without regaining consciousness."

At the Louisville Free Public Library, I located an article that corroborated this information in the *Courier-Journal* from the day after *The New York Times* piece ran. "Information reached this city Sunday night of the death of Mrs. Charles P. Robinson in New York. The deceased was widely known here, and she was a prominent member of society," it stated. Among other bits of information, it reported that she had "succumbed to death Sunday, after a long and painful illness." Nothing else at all about the manner of her death. Absolutely no mention whatsoever surfaced about the suicide – hardly surprising given that a family's position in Gilded Age society often afforded them the courtesies denied the lower echelons. The unpleasantries of stabbings, shootings, self-destruction and other mundane acts of violence were left to the poorer classes.

That many Louisvillians of the Gilded Age were spared the fact that poor Mrs. Robinson threw herself from a window in New York City is one thing, but whether this tragedy has anything to do with the apparent haunting at 1407 South Third Street is another. When I shared this bit of information with Bennet, he concluded that the suicide of the earlier resident's beloved wife must have tormented Charles P. Robinson well after he moved into the new mansion. "Perhaps his ghost cannot rest because he had no peace on earth," muses Bennet, "and that's why he cannot rest in death." One might think death ultimately provides the peace that was so elusive in life, but who knows? Specters are not known to be the most predictable of entities.

Chapter 8

THE ROCKING HORSE MANOR

Historic neighborhoods like Old Louisville lend themselves to bed and breakfast inns. With such an
impressive collection of Gilded Age mansions, it's
not surprising that innkeepers are inclined to throw open their doors to
welcome a steady stream of visitors in search of an up-close-and-person-
al experience in the historic district. Along with the Samuel Culbertson
Mansion and Campion House, several other grand mansions along the
old Millionaires Row have been converted to cozy B & Bs where guests
can enjoy a relaxing sojourn in the heart of this grand neighborhood.
One of them, a beautifully restored stone mansion in the Richardsonian
Romanesque style built around 1888, is found at 1022 South Third
Street. Today locals know it as the Rocking Horse Manor.

Like so many of the structures in Old Louisville, the interior
retains many of the typical features that defined life in a 19th-century
home. Ceilings soar almost thirteen feet above beautiful hardwood
floors, intricate hand-carved fireplace mantels, and original hand-sten-
ciled walls with pocket doors and ornate millwork. Lovely stained glass,
such as the colorful panes in the wainscoted wall next to the grand stairway in the foyer and in the elegant transoms in the second-floor windows, hints at the Old World charm enjoyed by the home's first residents.

Guests at this charming inn on Old Louisville's Millionaires Row have spotted a mysterious, regal figure on the sidewalk in front. Is it the specter of colorful character from the past?

Max Selliger, a prominent local distiller, built the home, and his family occupied it until the 1930s. Most recently, John Lysaght and Ricardo Bermudez have called it home, and during their tenure they've made thousands of overnight visitors feel at home. Given the large number of guests to the mansion, it's somewhat surprising that only a few people have reported ghostly encounters.

"As far as ghost stories, we haven't heard of any around here," say Lysaght and Bermudez, "but we're ready to hear any from previous guests with interesting encounters." Fortunately, two former visitors to the Rocking Horse Manor contacted me after reading my first book and shared with me their accounts of strange occurrences there.

Joe Leslie, a native of Cleveland, Ohio, spent a weekend at the bed and breakfast in early 2007. Despite the comfortable bed, the 45-year-old claims he had trouble falling asleep. "I don't know if I was all wired up from the trip or if I had eaten something that didn't agree with me, but I just couldn't fall asleep at first. I would start to get tired, but then I'd have the feeling of being watched. I got used to it after the first hour, but then the light on the bedside table flickered on and off several times. I turned it off, and it flashed on and off twice more after that, even though it wasn't on!"

Leslie claims that a faint noise could be heard in his room as well. "Several times, when the light went out, I could hear this soft rustling noise. It was like someone had shaken heavy curtains. Or like I could hear a woman's heavy dress swishing back and forth. It is really hard to describe the sound, but rustling fabric came to mind when I heard it. At one point I even thought I caught a glimpse of a woman in a big, fancy dress out of the corner of my eye."

Marty Green, a Kansas City businessman who spent a weekend at the Rocking Horse Manor in 2006, also reports a strange encounter with an elegantly dressed woman. "I have to tell you, I don't normally believe in this kind of stuff, but something very strange happened to me at that inn. I guess it was around two o'clock in the early morning and I was sleeping like a log. And I was having this really weird dream. There was this old woman standing at the foot of my bed, just staring at me. But she was almost smiling at me. She wasn't scary or anything."

According to Green, the thing that struck him about the vision

At the Rocking Horse Manor Bed & Breakfast lovely windows trimmed in stained glass afford wonderful views of Old Louisville's Millionaires Row. It is along this thoroughfare that guests have reported sightings of the famous ghost known as Lucinda.

was the woman's attire. "She was wearing some sort of sash across her upper body and had a tiara or something like that on the top of her head. She was wearing a big, old-fashioned dress, too, sort of like a ball gown. All I know is that she looked like an important woman from the Victorian times."

Green woke up a short time later and had a hard time falling back to sleep. "I kept thinking about that dream I had and couldn't get tired again. It was a really strange dream, one of those that seemed so real. So I just lay there in bed and decided to see what was on TV. Before I did that, though, I ran to the bathroom." On the way back to his bed, Green paused to take a look from one of the windows looking out onto Third Street. "Don't ask me why, I just wanted to see if anything was going on out there. So I leaned up against the window and was looking out, when I saw someone coming down the sidewalk."

In an instant, Green realized that the vision from his dream stood before him. "Crazy, right? I had to pinch myself to make sure I

Today's Rocking Horse Manor was built for bourbon baron Max Selliger in 1888. Its cozy dining room is ideal for a gourmet breakfast - and a ghost story or two.

wasn't still dreaming. I rubbed my eyes, and there she was, out on the street, the older woman in the ball gown I had dreamed about. She was just casually making her way down the sidewalk, going south. She didn't look up at me or anything, she just kept on walking like she was the only one in the world."

Despite the estimated 50 yards that separated him from the apparition, Green claims he could nonetheless make out details on the ghost such as the sparkling tiara. "I could see the banner or ribbon across her chest, and she had one of those old-time poofy skirts that kind of billowed out around her. I could see her as plain as day. That lasted for maybe ten seconds. Then, as she reached the end of the block, she disappeared. I know it sounds crazy, but that's what happened."

I shared this last account with several paranormal experts who live in Old Louisville and asked for their thoughts on the matter. They suggested two possible scenarios that might explain this alleged case of haunting. Assuming that what Mr. Green described is accurate, they feel he might have experienced a waking dream; in fact, he might have only dreamed that he awoke and got out of the bed, and witnessed the subsequent apparition.

The other theory involves the coincidental notion that he could have actually seen a woman wearing a tiara walking down Third Street in the wee hours of the morning. Old Louisville is a neighborhood known for its Bohemian characters, and, suffice to say, stranger things have been seen here.

Could the rustling of the invisible fabric heard on the previous occasion be the swaying of the apparition's dress as she skulked about in Joe Leslie's room at the Rocking Horse Manor? It could be. Personally, I like to think that the apparition spotted in front of Lysaght and Bermudez's bed and breakfast is none other than the ghost of Lucinda, a famed character from Old Louisville's Gilded Age who made frequent appearances up and down Millionaires Row. To learn more about Old Louisville's most regal lady, read on.

For information about the Rocking Horse Manor Bed & Breakfast, call (502) 583-0408 or visit www.rockinghorse-bb.com.

ABOUT THE QUEEN OF AMERICA

Old Louisville of the Gilded Age counted as a bastion of elegance and refinement on the edge of the frontier. In its lavish parlors and drawing rooms, emphasis was placed on manners and the correct way of doing things, and over time a tight-knit community with its own customs and caste system evolved. Manual laborers such as bricklayers and deliverymen occupied the lower rungs of the social ladder and right above them fell household servants and day workers. In the middle came those with professions such as teachers, bookkeepers and clerks, and at the very top sat a substantial echelon of the moneyed class. Some of its members came from old Kentucky families of wealth, but many of them were merchants who derived their fortunes from the booming industries that had sprouted up to supply city residents with the necessities. Shoe manufacturer, oil refiner, furniture producer, hardware merchant, carriage maker, wholesale saddler – these are just some of the professions listed for early residents of Old Louisville. An examination of early city directories, however, shows that a large number of distillers, tobacco executives, and – later on – racetrack associates populated the neighborhood. It was these, the kings of industry, who shaped the cultural landscape of the neighborhood, and it's only natural that the very wealthiest residents came to be seen as local royalty.

A substantial number of Louisvillians actually achieved regal status through marriage to members of the European nobility. In early November 1900 Miss Grace Carr married Lord Newborough, "head of one of the oldest Welsh families in existence," in the Savoy Chapel in London, and at the end of that same month *The New York Times* announced: "Another Louisville girl will marry a member of the Continental nobility." The wedding, between Miss Lillian May Langham and Baron Herman Speck von Sternburg, took place on December 5 in London.

In 1901 Miss Patti Ellison became Lady Ross after her sensational marriage to Sir Charles Henry Augustus Lockhart Ross, the ninth baronet of Balnagowan, Scotland, at her family's home on Fourth Avenue. And in 1903 papers across the country buzzed with the news that Lady Newborough's sister, Mrs. Alice Carr Chauncey, was set to become a peeress with her marriage to Lord Rosebery, the ex-premier of England. In addition, *The New York Times* reported in 1912 that heirs had settled the $6 million estate of the late Baroness von Zedtwitz, "formerly Miss Mary Elizabeth Caldwell of Louisville." It seemed that her sister, the Marquis Monstiers-Merinville, had also done well for herself in the marriage business.

Given the number of aristocratic women from the area, would anyone wonder that the ghost of an elderly dame in regal attire has been seen promenading along Millionaires Row? In life, they called her Lucinda, and she was a regular sight on the streets of Old Louisville during the 1880s, when the neighborhood teamed with visitors to the Southern Exposition. Although not much is known about her personal life, people such as Max Selliger had always considered her a somewhat eccentric character. Sadly, as her eccentricity increased, her grasp on reality loosened and somewhere along the line, Lucinda proclaimed herself the "Queen of America."

The New York Times picked up on Lucinda's antics in 1885 and reported the details of her most recent appearance on October 30. "An old lady, with a remarkable appearance and bearing, swept into the Circuit Court this morning with queenly grace. She was under the escort of a couple of policemen, and was given a seat in front of the jury. This was a celebrate crank, Lucinda, Queen of America," it wrote. "For several years, she has been a conspicuous character, and she was in the habit of appearing in public places in regal attire. She would go to the Galt House and ask for the King and everywhere she was the same queenly personage."

It appeared, however, that Queen Lucinda had some problems in her kingdom. She feared a plot to assassinate her and became convinced that someone wanted to usurp her throne. When she engaged a local attorney to bar the would-be usurper, he jokingly informed her that "the Attorney-General of the United States was the proper person to take steps. The next thing heard of her she was in Washington besieging President Arthur. . . . Since that time, she has issued long weekly proclamations, sending them to all the newspaper offices."

But her antics took a turn for the worse when the 74-year-old barricaded herself in her rooms on Sixth Street, terrified that the assassins had come to do their dirty work. After a minor scuffle, the authorities hauled her off to jail and then to a courtroom to discuss the issue of her sanity. According to reports in *The New York Times*, the regent reported to all assembled that the country was well governed and that the threat of assassination had passed. "Her son was Emperor and Bob Ingersoll was King. Mr. McDonald, of Texas, was President. . . . She was of course adjudged a lunatic."

What happened to Lucinda after the courts committed her to the insane asylum has yet to be discovered, but her spirit appears to be alive and well in Old Louisville.

Chapter 9

THE COLUMBINE

everal blocks from the Rocking Horse Manor sits another of Old Louisville's bed and breakfast inns. Prominent lumber merchant Clarence Mengel constructed the mansion around 1896 at 2105 South Third Street (currently number 1707), and extensive restoration almost a hundred years later converted the home to the Columbine Bed & Breakfast. Opulent, yet gracious and inviting at the same time, the interior of the mansion radiates a sense of grandeur that has nonetheless faded in many other Old Louisville architectural masterpieces of the Gilded Age.

The home's original occupants, the Mengels, enjoyed some renown for their family's local furniture empire, and Clarence's reputation as the "Mahogany King" shows itself in the extensive use of wood throughout the house. Each room, such as the inviting double parlor on the bottom floor, displays elaborate and detailed examples of hardwood flooring, and wainscoted walls on the first floor shine with rare Honduran mahogany. Eight-foot sliding pocket doors separate the parlor from the dining room. Because quarter-sawn oak trims one room and mahogany the other, each side of the laminated doors features wood that matches the room it faces when the doors are closed.

In the elegant foyer, a graceful staircase sweeps up to a spacious landing before splitting and doubling back to the second-story corridor.

Guests to the Columbine Bed & Breakfast are greeted by this impressive Greek Revival facade built around 1896 for Clarence Mengel, the "Mahogany King."

The landing boasts a magnificent stained-glass window with a built-in, hand-carved window seat where pensive observers can enjoy a leisurely moment basked in golden, honey hues as sunlight filters its way through panes of amber crystal. The third floor, originally the gentleman's billiard room and lounge, offers glimpses of angled rooflines, original pocket doors and the home's characteristic half-moon window visible in the pediment of the façade. Outside, two porches and manicured grounds round out the overall appeal of the Columbine. Little wonder it has become a favored stop for overnight visitors to Old Louisville.

Rich May and Bob Goldstein have enjoyed sharing the beautiful mansion with numerous guests from around the world since they became owners of the venerable inn. Some of their guests – as expected in America's most haunted neighborhood – have had ghostly encounters there.

May and Goldstein, however, have never experienced anything out of the ordinary themselves, and they remain firmly convinced that absolutely nothing of a paranormal nature is afoot in the old house. Nonetheless, the two readily concede that now and then visitors to the mansion report strange occurrences that suggest supernatural forces might be at play after all . . . at least in the minds of those who would welcome paranormal encounters.

Whether or not these claims arise as the result of bona fide ghostly encounters is another thing, however. Active imaginations and wishful thinking often increase the frequency of these reports, but that's not to say that real spectral phenomena couldn't be stirring the air at the Columbine. After all, a home such as the former Mengel mansion –with countless visitors over more than 110 years – could be prone to phantom activity.

Colette Angstrom, a native of Leicester, England, and self-proclaimed "sensitive," recalled her visit to the Columbine during a recent telephone interview. "I adore bed and breakfasts and Louisville has quite a number of them. My favorite is the Columbine because of those wonderful columns in the front that look like something out of *Gone with the Wind*. You walk in that spacious front foyer and see that marvelous set of stairs with that absolutely radiant stained glass, and it really transports you back in time. It's a brilliant addition to the neighborhood."

It was in the foyer where Angstrom received what she terms her first "psychic impressions" about the house. "I was made immediately aware of several strong presences on the property," she explains, "and I

*Are ghosts on the menu in the dining room at the lovely Columbine Bed &
Breakfast? Although sightings are very rare, some guests have reported strange
apparitions and floating orbs in this part of the mansion.*

was shown a glimpse of the past. It could be explained as a series of quick flashes on a movie screen, but all the images were colorless. I distinctly saw two individuals descending the stairs in front of me. Then I was drawn to an impression I was getting to my right. What I saw appeared to be a family sitting down to tea in the front room. I saw a gentleman and two ladies, one of them older than the other. Perhaps it was the original family who lived there. In any case, they were all attired in clothing that appeared to be late Victorian in style. I didn't sense any negative energy whatsoever, but it is indeed a place with a high concentration of white light. I get the feeling someone – or maybe more – is watching over the place."

Other guests at the mansion have reported similar experiences. "I was getting ready to take a stroll around the neighborhood," says Michelle Stainsbury, a Massachusetts resident who prefers to stay at the Columbine when business brings her to town. "I was in the foyer waiting for my husband. He came down the steps and as I looked up, I noticed there was someone coming down the stairs behind him. A woman in an old dress. Then she was gone. My husband saw the look on my face and asked what the matter was. When I told him what I had seen, he said he was the only one upstairs – there was no one else in the inn at the time."

On another occasion, Stainsbury reported apparitions in the dining room "The next day, as I walked to the front door, past the dining room to my left, I looked over and saw two women behind the table and in front of the fireplace. They looked up at me like I startled them and then they disappeared. The strange thing was the way they were dressed." According to Stainsbury, the duo had all the trappings of well-dressed women of the late 19th century. "The thing that stuck out the most was that they wore bustled skirts. It was like I stumbled into a scene from the past. I don't know who they were, but that's what I saw."

A search of neighborhood records offers no clues as to why spectral scenes of past domesticity might linger on in the Clarence Mengel mansion, and some have suggested that a residual view of the past has imprinted itself on the historical veneer of the property. In short, the Columbine counts as another of those Old Louisville structures that throbs with place memory, and nothing else.

I stopped by one day to pay Rich May a visit and take some pictures of the mansion. Since I had heard stories about the grand stairway, I made sure to take lots of photographs there. When I got home and took a closer look at the pictures, I noticed that in one them, two distinct orbs could be seen on the staircase. Orbs are spherical shapes that often appear in pictures taken in areas of reportedly high supernatural activity. I don't know that they indicate the presence of ghosts in the Columbine, but I did find it interesting that of the 50 pictures I took, orbs only showed up on one, and that was one of the staircase.

On the other hand, there are those who suggest that the appearance of orbs in photos at the Columbine substantiates the rumors of spectral activity there. In doing subsequent research, I came across people who put forth the notion that a spell cast on the Mengel family many, many years ago accounts for any number of strange happenings in homes where the Mengels have resided. Sandra Caudill, a resident of Sixth Street, claims a nearby tree ties into a legendary family curse. For details, read on about the spookiest tree in the neighborhood.

For information about the Columbine Bed & Breakfast, call (502) 635 5000 or visit online at www.thecolumbine.com.

ABOUT ORBS

Orbs are apparently transparent balls of light that manifest themselves in photographs taken in areas of purported supernatural activity. Many believe them to be actual ghosts or spirits in the spherical forms of light, while others believe they are the result of nearby energy sources manifesting themselves in different forms. Skeptics suggest that orbs come about as nothing more than water droplets on the camera lense or dust particles that become visible under the right circumstances. Although I have only captured orbs on several occasions, I find it intriguing that they only appeared in pictures taken in places that were supposedly haunted – and where the place could have used a good dusting. May and Goldstein seem to run a spotless establishment, however, so who knows what could have caused their orbs.

Orbs surround the Columbine stairs. Orbs are said to appear as a manifestation of supernatural energy, however many believe they are nothing more than floating particles of dust.

ABOUT THE WITCH'S TREE

Even though the Mengels often looked to forests in exotic locations like Honduras, Mexico and Africa for their millworking needs, the lush areas surrounding their Old Louisville homes yielded a steady supply of luxurious and sturdy native woods that were recylcled into trim for traditional Kentucky homes. More than a century later, rich specimens of locally grown oak, maple, walnut and cherry can still be found in many of the trimmings that adorn the surviving mansions of Old Louisville's Gilded Age. When visitors walk through the neighborhood today, towering trees hint at the abundance the Kentucky countryside must have presented to early settlers and builders. During the warm spring and summer months, the dappled shade of their canopies provide welcome relief from the sun, but when the chill winds of winter and fall rob them of their leaves, these trees and their bare branches can take on a more sinister appearance. A times, some of them can look downright spooky.

At the northwest corner of Park and Sixth Street in Old Louisville stands a gnarled old tree known by locals as the "Spooky Tree." Others call it the "Witch's Tree." A jagged canopy of dead branches juts out to the north, and large, barky warts cover the twisted trunk, adding to its scary appearance. Known as burls, these rounded growths often appear on tree trunks or branches, and they arise when a deformity arises in the wood grain. According to arborists, burls usually occur when trees undergo some form of stress induced by either environmental or human agents. In Old Louisville, however, most people don't subscribe to this notion; the strange growths on the spooky old tree came about as the result of witchcraft.

Despite the scientific and technological advances of the 19th century, many parts of Louisville's largest city held on to old superstitions, and belief in curses, black magic and witches was commonplace. Given that the riverboat and rail connections to New Orleans and other points in the South ensured a constant stream of followers of the voodoo arts, these voodoo (also known as "hoodoo" in some parts) practioners kept the Old Louisville neighborhood hopping with supernatural action. The Witch's Tree emerged as a meeting point for many of these dabblers in the black arts.

According to local legend, the tree known as the Witch's Tree started its life as a majestic, towering maple that sprang up practically overnight in the late 1800s when the Dumesnil family still owned the land. Famed for the lovely flower beds and hedgerows that graced the grounds of their estate, the Dumesnils once maintained an adjacent tract of land dedicated to the cultivation of ornamental shrubs, myriad rose bushes and a wide variety of flowers. Locals named it the Dumesnil Botanical Gardens, and it became a popular destination for visitors in search of a bit of rest and relaxation from the hustle and bustle of life in a 19th-century metropolis. During the warm months of the great Southern Exposition from 1883 to 1887, its shady pathways and fragrant blooms provided welcome relief from the Kentucky sun to thousands of visitors from around the world.

When word later got out that the Dumesnils planned to sell their beautiful gardens to the city and that planners would develop the land to construct houses, many people in the neighborhood were heartbroken to think they would lose their treasured botanical gardens. The most distraught of all, however, was a coven of local witches. The imposing tree, with its perfectly straight trunk, had become the prefered gathering spot for nightly rituals where they mixed potions and cast spells on those who incurred their wrath or curried their favor. A terrible storm had almost toppled their favorite tree once, and they were not ready to lose it.

By most accounts, problems began in the spring of 1889 as locals began preparations for their annual May Day celebrations. Although few people today still celebrate May 1 as the advent of spring, Victorian America saw it as a symbolic banishment of the cold winter weather and, as such, a great cause for festivities. And integral to any traditional May Day celebration was a dance around the maypole. Early Americans, following the traditions of their European ancestors, usually erected maypoles of maple, hawthorn or birch, and then festooned the tall pole with flowers, greenery and large wreaths with long, colored ribbons suspended from the top. Children would then perform dances around the maypole, their rehearsed steps resulting in the weave of elaborate patterns in the ribbons.

Legend holds that this gnarled tree at the corner of Park and Sixth in Old Louisville was - and still is - a favorite meeting spot for local witches.

Given their connection to the lumber industry, it fell to the Mengels to organize the neighborhood May Day celebrations every year. With tons of logs at their disposal, they usually sent their employees to pick out the tallest and straightest one to be erected and decorated. In 1889, however, the Mengels decide to cut down a local tree, the beautiful maple at the corner of Sixth and Park. Although it counted as a joyous celebration, the local witches were less than thrilled to learn that their beloved maple had been singled out for its flawless shape and impressive height.

At the end of April, they learned, their tree would be cut down, shorn of its branches and then decorated for the local May Day celebration. The witches got together and posted a parchment note on their tree. Addressed to Mr. Mengel, it read:

> This tree shall stand and not be cut,
> lest a lesson be paid to you, the Dunce
> Who hatched this hare-brained plan.
> If our tree should fall, then Fate will call
> On this city in eleven months.

The notice hung on the majestic maple for more than a month and became tattered and torn as the elements battered and blew. Although the Mengels were informed of the warning, no one paid much attention to it. The parchment eventually disintegrated and faded away altogether. It seems people didn't take witches as seriously as they had in the olden days after all.

On the last day of April, when two woodsmen from the Mengel factory cut down the great tree, it was said that a mournful wail was heard ensuing from the nearby forests. By the next day, the lovely maple had been resurrected in a different location, decorated with fresh flowers, colorful ribbons and boughs of greenery. Mr. Mengel officiated at the ceremony and the celebrations went off without a hitch.

After the May Day festivities, the trunk was dried, cut and burned in a great Whitsuntide bonfire. By the time the heat of summer arrived, most had forgotten about the witches' warning and the beautiful maple tree. When the winds of fall and winter starting whipping through the neighborhood, rumors had it that the coven had moved to a distant forest where they had resumed their nightly gatherings and castings of spells. When townspeople began planning for the next May Day celebration in April, the witches' cursed had slipped from memory. Not a soul had an inkling of the tragedy that lay ahead when the eleventh month neared its end.

On the evening of March 28, 1890, the most destructive tornado in the history of Louisville roared in from the west and destroyed a large portion of the city. Within five minutes, more than 600 buildings – including some 500 homes, 10 tobacco warehouses, three schools and the downtown train station – had been shattered like kindling. It was also reported that the winds had wreaked havoc at the Mengels largest lumber works.

In the end, 100 lives were lost as well and weeks passed before anybody thought about that year's May Day festivities. Residents in the neighborhood around the Dumesnil Botanical Gardens reported that when the winds of the storm had subsided, they noticed that a gnarled and twisted old tree had magically sprouted up on the spot formerly occupied by the majestic old maple. When word got out that the devastating tornado had first been spotted on Maple Street, locals remembered the witches and their warning not to cut down their beloved tree. From that point forward, the locals refused to use maples for their annual maypole, and rumors soon spread that the coven of witches had returned to conduct their nightly rituals. They still frequent the neighborhood today, although they only cast evil spells on very rare occasions, and no one dares cut down any more trees of any kind for fear of incurring their wrath. To this day, people say the gnarled old tree violently rattles its brittle and twisted branches in warning whenever a tornado threatens the neighborhood.

Or whenever a member of the Mengel family walks by.

Chapter 10

THE RUSSELL HOUSTON MANSION

Although many of Old Louisville's most impressive mansions of the Gilded Age can be found along the stretch of South Third Street known as Millionaires Row, splendid homes can be found throughout the entire neighborhood. Given that Ormsby Avenue at one time marked the southernmost extension of the original city, it has many of the earliest and largest homes of those in the area. The comfortable upper-middle-class enclaves of First and Second streets both have impressive residences known for their innovative architectural styles, and St. James and Belgravia Court mansions and town homes have come to epitomize the charm and elegance of Old Louisville's Victorian past. But if one street in Old Louisville rivals South Third Street for the size and grandeur of its Gilded Age masterpieces, it is Fourth Street.

Once the most exclusive address for the city's wealthiest merchants, downtown Fourth Avenue – as it started out – transformed itself from a pastoral residential district to a bustling center of commerce and entertainment for much of the 19th and 20th centuries. Although no visible reminders of the once-vibrant housing scene that characterized the street north of Broadway remain, the southern stretch that passes through Old Louisville boasts quite a number of spacious and elegant mansions from the city's golden age. One of the most striking of these

Judge Russell Houston and his family lived in this magnificent red brick mansion overlooking Central Park. The ghost of a former tutor for the children has been said to haunt the lovely mansion, which is now a bed and breakfast.

sits at the corner of Fourth and Park in the heart of Old Louisville. Known as the Russell Houston Mansion, 1332 South Fourth Street is one of the most inviting and elegant Victorian queens in the neighborhood, and like so many homes in Old Louisville, it has its share of stories and legends.

Construction on the storied 7,400-square-foot mansion for Russell Houston, president of the L&N Railroad, started in the mid 1880s, a heady time for Louisville because of the excitement and national publicity generated by the famous Southern Exposition. Elements of the popular Richardsonian Romanesque style can be found on the exterior of the eye-catching red-brick masterpiece designed by prominent Kentucky architect Maury Mason. Historians William Morgan and Samuel H. Thomas have described its appearance as "a picturesque massing of brick into a powerful composition of tremendous originality," making special note of the highly decorative red stone trim, sills, quoining, belt courses, lintels and columns that unify the lovely façade. A jaunty turret juts from the south-facing corner and a lone dormer perches on the steep-pitched roof over a graceful third-floor balcony.

In the spacious foyer, arriving guests notice inviting coffered ceilings and an impressive stairway that gently wraps its way around to the second floor. The one-of-a-kind fireplace in the dining room features an embedded window in a double-flue chimney with an enviable view of the green heart of Old Louisville, the Olmsted-designed Central Park that replaced old DuPont Square in 1905. And in addition to the many charming details and antique furnishings that fill the interior spaces, rumor has it that a resident haunt adds character to the home of Russell Houston. Here the ghost of Annie Whipple lives on in local legend.

Tall and schoolmarmly, the sad specter has been seen ascending and descending the lovely, curving staircase at the Houston residence, seemingly lost in thought over a terrible mistake she made over a hundred years ago.

According to local lore, Annie Whipple one time worked in the lovely brick mansion that overlooks Central Park. A mysterious widow who had recently arrived from New England, she taught the children of the neighborhood elite and became the tutor at the Houston home, where she enjoyed a position of authority and respect. That is, until one day, when she started to dabble in the practice of the black arts.

Although I have yet to locate such a document, Annie Whipple supposedly wrote a type of confession, as it were, on her deathbed, and it went something like this:

"The memory still haunts me. One of my charges, a bright little girl named Elizabeth, and a dear, sweet soul, fell ill with yellow fever in the fall of the year of 1892, and when doctors could do nothing to alleviate her suffering and imminent death, I resorted to the world of spirits to find her relief. Little did I know it would be my undoing.

"I had read in the newspapers that popular opinion had it that one could actually commune with the dead, and many a respected scientist had reported much success in his attempts to correspond with the long departed. So I decided to embark upon a sojourn of my own making in which I would seek counsel from the other side of the living. Under advisement from an old African woman who knew of such things and witchery, I learned the secrets of séance and was given over to finding a cure for my dear girl's misery.

"On a night, when the moon was full, and when frost tipped the breeze with cold, I went to the dark-paneled study and commenced in my intercourse. In the weeks prior to dear Elizabeth's infection with the fever, a well-known and revered doctor of the medical arts by the name of Dr. Anderson had breathed his last in the throes of old age and had peacefully slipped from this world to the next. The wise old man was said to have talents that could restore to health the most hopelessly infirm, and I transpired to divine his secrets.

"I lit a solitary white candle, gathered paper and writing utensils and sat at the table in the study. I sprinkled over its surface a magic powder given me by the old African woman before I intoned a prayer to conjure up the spirit of Dr. Anderson, and an eerie hush soon fell over the room. Although I could see naught, it seemed a presence hovered at my side, and I was sure as day that Dr. Anderson stood ready to assist. 'My dear Dr. Anderson,' I pleaded, 'my sweet Elizabeth is taken with the fever, and only you can save her life. Please advise me so that I may prolong her stay on this plane.'

"With that, a deep trance came over me and my head slumped.

Unawares, my hand lifted a pen and dipped its tip in ink before scrawling something across the paper in front of me. When I awoke and beheld the message, it seemed that a medical prescription had magically appeared before me.

"Early the next morning, joyful that I had the cure at hand, I ran to a nearby apothecary and had the receipt filled and then returned swiftly to this abode where I administered the potion to my young charge. As I waited at her side, and as minutes turned to hours, it became apparent that the medicine had not served its purpose and only worsened young Elizabeth's condition. She fell into a deep sleep, and the doctor who was summoned pronounced that she would surely expire by the coming dawn.

"Such devastation I had never experienced before! I ran to the table in the study and sprinkled the magic powder over a sheet of paper before I once again summoned the shade of Dr. Anderson. 'My good physician,' I implored. 'Please return and render assistance. Young Elizabeth is now sure for the grave, and I cannot stand it she should perish.'

"Once again, a hush came upon the room, and I was entranced, my limp hand seizing the pen and scrawling out a message from the other side. Upon awakening, I was horrified to read its meaning. The chilling words read: You fool! I am not Dr. Anderson!

"I fell in a heap to the floor, insensitive to all external consciousness, and they took my limp body up to my room, where I lay in fitful slumber till the dawn broke. When I finally woke, it was only for a moment, as fever had wracked my body with pain and delirium, but with happiness I saw Elizabeth, flushed and glowing, who stood before me and smiled.

"What wicked phantasms had tricked me so, I cannot say. But before I knew it, the light began to fade, and I summoned paper and pen with which to write my sad tale and give warning to those who would tempt the Fates as had I. Now I lie here, destined for the grave, yet exceedingly glad that the young girl's life has been spared, knowing that mine will be forfeited in exchange."

By the time the sun set, Annie Whipple lay dead. But since that day, local legend holds that her specter is fated to tread the halls in the mansion where the Houstons once lived, reminiscing the day she dabbled in the black arts and surrendered the life she enjoyed on earth.

Although my initial research on the legend of Annie Whipple turned up absolutely no substantiation for this haunting, I did make some interesting discoveries concerning the history of spiritualism and what some consider the "black arts" in this area. Although the concept of communing with the deceased undoubtedly extends back to the beginnings of humankind and receives no small amount of comment in the Bible, most agree that modern-day spiritualism traces its roots to 1848, when the Fox sisters reportedly made irrefutable contact with a ghost in their home in upstate New York. Word of the phenomenon soon spread, and within a decade or two it had taken hold on the imaginations of those in this country and abroad.

Among the early cases of spiritualist activity in the Louisville area is a tongue-in-cheek story in the *Courier-Journal* of 1869 about the "Very Latest in Spiritual Sensation." It reported: "The latest wonder in Jeffersonville spiritualism is the furnishing of money for shows and buggy riding by spirits to mortals." The specter of Mr. Bud Morgan, deceased several years prior, it explained, had made "its headquarters at the residence of Mr. Keigwin, and, it is alleged, that he is daily and almost hourly engaged in conversation with the different members of the family, who converse with him as freely and familiarly as if he were in the flesh." Not only was the deceased generous in his otherworldly correspondence, the piece also reported that members of the Keigwin family enjoyed the good fortune of communing with a spirit who often provided them with money to buy circus tickets and carriage rides.

Spiritualism often received scathing rebukes by the established clergy and warnings against the evils of "divining and sorcery." *The New York Times* of March 31, 1872, picked up on a sensational report about "The Lady of Louisville," against whom "a Presbyterian Church in Louisville, Ky. has instituted proceedings" . . . for being "understood to be a believer in 'spiritualism.'" After making the assertion that forbidden intercourse with the dead stemmed from Jewish law – and as such, the Christians of Louisville were not bound by "the multitudinous provisions of the Mosaic code" – the writer offered a somewhat liberal piece of advice for the times: "Let the Jewish law, which is supposed to forbid intercourse with the dead – though it is by no means certain that such is its true meaning – be treated in the same spirit in which we treat the Jewish prohibition of pork. We hold it wrong to eat measly pork, but right to eat wholesome and tender corn-fed pork. In like manner, let association with wicked and morally measly spirits be deprecated, but let us concede the right of any good man to converse with good spirits – if he can." In conclusion, the commentator argued that most good spirits, as a rule, occupied themselves with rather mundane communications anyway, so any influence they could exert on the lady would most likely "be to provoke in her that meditative calmness immediately preceding healthy and innocent sleep."

I also came across an interesting article in *The New York Times* of July 30, 1871, that circulated a story first reported in the *New Albany Ledger*, which told of a supposedly possessed woman in Indiana, just across the river from Louisville. What really caught my attention when I quickly scanned the report about "the bewitched woman" was the mention of a "witch doctor" by the name of Dr. Anderson who "lived in the city."

It seems, therefore, that a Dr. Anderson did indeed exist, lending some degree of credence to the story about Annie Whipple and her ill-fated attempts at communication with the dead. Like so many of the legends and unsubstantiated stories in Old Louisville, reports of this ghostly encounter suggest at least a tenuous connection with the past, a correlation borne out in neighborhood folklore and modern oral traditions.

If anyone needs convincing that the specter of Annie Whipple haunts the grand stairway at the Russell Houston home, don't fret. The red-brick mansion at the corner of Park and South Fourth has been converted to a comfortable inn, and owners Herb and Gayle Warren welcome overnight guests to come and check it out for themselves. Known as the Inn at the Park, the old Houston place now counts as one of the most popular B&Bs in the neighborhood. Although there haven't been any very recent sightings of a willowy wraith in a high-wasted skirt and lacy white blouse on the graceful, curving stairway in the foyer, believers claim it's just a matter of time before she reappears for another round of lessons.

For more information about Old Louisville's Inn at the Park, call (502) 638-0045 or go online at www.innatpark.com.

ABOUT FOURTH STREET'S ONE-ARMED SPECTERS

In a neighborhood as storied and historic as Old Louisville, it is only appropriate to expect a wealth of legend and lore. Once a story has taken root in the soil, it becomes part of the local fabric and no amount of skepticism can dislodge it. But when the occasional historical tidbit surfaces to lend credence to events that have been chalked up to the stuff of urban legend, one can only scratch one's head and wonder if the information counts as substantiation of the reports.

For many years, residents and passers-by on South Fourth Street have reported unsettling encounters with no less than two alleged ghosts with the same unfortunate distinguishing feature, namely that of a missing limb. One, a scruffy-looking man of advanced age in a Civil War uniform and cloak, has been spotted shuffling down the street near the Russell Houston home. The other, an older black woman in petticoats with a bandana around her head, haunts the same stretch of road. Both of them have empty sleeves where one of their arms should be, and their ghosts appear to have some precedent in Louisville history.

The male entity, according to local lore, is none other than the Old Colonel himself, the real-life role model for the Little Colonel in the series of the same name that brought the Samuel Culbertson family no small amount of fame and recognition. Author Annie Fellows Johnston gives the following account of the old soldier in her 1929 autobiography *Land of the Little Colonel*:

> Along this street one summer morning, nearly thirty years ago, came stepping an old Confederate Colonel. Every one greeted him deferentially. He was always pointed out to new comers. Some people called attention to him because he had given his right arm to the lost cause, some because they thought he resembled Napoleon, and others because they had some amusing tale to tell of his eccentricities. He was always clad in white duck in the summer, and was wrapped in a picturesque military cape in the winter.

It is the caped figure that has been reported on numerous occasions in the neighborhood. Mary Ann Culbertson describes herself as "one of those out-of-towners who loves Old Louisville" and she claims to have caught a glimpse of the mysterious figure herself. "We had just arrived in Old Louisville for the first time. I was a little overwhelmed so we drove around to get oriented. I noticed a figure on one of the benches on Fourth Street, but when we got nearer I had a better view and no one was sitting there. It seemed to be someone wearing a black hat and a cape, but as my glimpse was very brief I can't say for sure." The sighting occurred in front of 1469 South Fourth Street, less than two blocks from the Russell Houston Mansion and right behind the Samuel Culbertson Mansion.

On a comprehensive and helpful Web site devoted to Annie Fellows Johnston and the Little Colonel stories, the Samuel Culbertson Mansion offers some intriguing details about the Old Colonel. According to local records, his real name was George Washington Weissinger Jr. and he had indeed served as a colonel in the Confederate forces. And just as portrayed in the Little Colonel stories, Colonel Weissinger had lost his right arm, something confirmed in Civil War records from the battle of Sugar Creek, Arkansas, in March 1862. Although he died on February 24, 1903, at the age of 66 at St. Joseph's Infirmary – then located on Fourth Street between Broadway and Chestnut at the present site of the Palace Theater – they took the body to his brother Harry's house in Old Louisville. Old city directories show that Harry Weissinger lived near the corner of Fourth and Oak, just a block away from the Russell Houston home. According to newspaper accounts, a well-attended funeral took place around the corner at St. Louis Bertrand Catholic Church before they interred the Old Colonel at Cave Hill Cemetery.

Substantiation for the existence of the armless old black woman is much harder to come by, but legend suggests that she was the same "old African woman" consulted by Annie Whipple in her quest to commune with the dead. Wanda Kenwick, a lifetime resident of Louisville's West End, remembers her grandmother telling stories of "a hoo-doo woman called 'Old Josephine' who was known for casting spells and reading fortunes."

Although she began her career in the occult with both upper appendages, Old Josephine had an unfortunate run-in with less-tolerant individuals later on in life, and this supposedly led to her ghost's one-armed status. "Mamaw told us some little church nearby got all upset because Josephine wouldn't quit with her magic and stuff, and they kept on warning her and warning her, and she still kept doing what she wanted till one day she got in trouble." Kenwick says angry churchgoers took matters into their own hands. "They got her one night, tied her to a tree in the cemetery and cut off the arm she used for doing her conjuring."

Whether the poor woman died of her injuries and decided to torment the neighborhood in revenge has yet to be determined, but, to me, it seems as good a reason as any to haunt a locale. That she existed at all hasn't been proven, but some folklorists agree that where there's paranormal smoke, there's historical fire.

I encountered one highly disturbing article during my research that has fanned the flames of possibility in my mind. I was researching a completely different topic late one night, when I happened across a tiny piece that ran in the *Atlanta Constitution* more than a hundred years ago:

DECAYING ARM
ON DOOR KNOB

Limb of Negro Woman
Left at Front of
Louisville Mansion.

Louisville, KY., March 17. – The decomposed arm of a negro woman was found suspended from the residence of Mrs. K.M. Bacon, 1006 South Fourth avenue, a fashionable residence, at 10 o'clock this morning.

Police officers cut down the arm and called the coroner.

As if that weren't odd enough, I noticed that the article ran in 1903, just weeks after the Old Colonel had passed away not too far down the street. Gruesome coincidence or paranormal proof, the notion that two individuals with severed limbs had some connection with the same short stretch of Fourth Street around the very same time does give one pause.

If two armless specters really lurk in the shadows between the grand mansions that still dot Fourth Street, I hope they've had the pleasure to make their respective acquaintances. Maybe they can offer each other some solace, if not some actual physical support. But wouldn't it be a cynical twist of spectral fate if they both had lost their right arms and couldn't at least walk arm-in-arm down the grand boulevard they once knew?

Although I haven't made their acquaintance, I will continue to stroll the streets in search of more ghosts of the Gilded Age, or whatever age might want to reveal more secrets, hoping I can finagle my way beyond the front doors of more allegedly haunted mansions. I hear the Roaring Twenties were a great time in Old Louisville. I'm sure the spirits of long-dead flappers, bootleggers and gangsters have some great stories to tell. Stay tuned!

AFTERWORD

David Dominé always had a talent for entertaining. It's good to see this talent alive and well today in *Haunts of Old Louisville: Gilded Age Ghosts and Haunted Mansions in America's Spookiest Neighborhood.* When I met David Dominé over fifteen years ago at the Seelbach Hotel, where we both worked together in the Oakroom Restaurant, his generous spirit and willingness to share his knowledge always put me in mind of another writer associated with the Seelbach Hotel.

Looking out over the Ohio River, F. Scott Fitzgerald, saw a shining light in Indiana that inspired him to write *The Great Gatsby.* Its main character is described as the type who likes to give presents on his birthday and these traits are apparent in David's benevolent nature, as he too, hands out presents to those entering his door for his frequent celebrations. His parties are indicative of yesteryear with bright conversation, games and – yes! – ghost stories. After hearing of one such gathering, my father discernedly exclaimed: "People don't entertain like that anymore!"

Now, David entertains with his *Ghosts of Old Louisville* series, not only recounting ghostly encounters, but researching the history of beautiful, old homes. Recently, he listened with an open ear as I told about an odd evening at an Old Louisville apartment where I lived while attending U of L.

The day before, I had discovered a huge file of old wives tales and witchcraft at the library on York Street. As I read, I came across a warning against sweeping in the night because you might sweep up spirits. I promptly forgot about it, but the next evening before the sun had set, I decided to sweep the dead leaves from my front porch. After several passes with the broom, I glanced up to see an old black man gliding by, the setting sun shining at his back. In an eerie Cajun accent, he said: "It is bad to sweep in the night."

I stopped sweeping. "I know. I just read that yesterday," I responded. "But I'm just getting rid of a few more leaves."

The old man stopped short, turned his head in my direction and repeated in his thick accent. "But it is bad to sweep in the night."

I felt mesmerized by his glare and after a pause, I said: "You're right. I'm done." I turned to go inside but as I looked back, no one was there. Curiosity made me walk to the sidewalk and glance both ways, but I saw no one. I got a chill that evening, but it was years later when I realized I must have swept him up.

I don't know where the Cajun man came from, but David encourages me to keep looking. And I've been inspired to research the history and haunts of my grandmother's old farmhouse where I now live in Bloomfield, Kentucky. Strange things have always happened here, but when my brother started some recent renovations, it seems that the occurrences increased. A door slammed in my face after I complained about its slow annoying creak. As well, a pantry door would not close and felt as if a rubber ball were in the way. A mysterious shadow – Is it a lady in a long skirt with a long dark braid? – has appeared in the halls to check on my daughter Hannah so many times that she's stopped asking "Was that just you, mommy?"

I don't know what things might be afoot in my old house, but Socrates was right when he said: "It's a wise man who admits to knowing nothing." David's objective and inquiring nature inspires and invites us to be open-minded enough to listen, research, and consider that our own senses are perhaps not failing us when we question them, but rather enlighten us. He gives us a guide to ponder our past and appreciate the present as we walk with him through Old Louisville. I'm personally looking forward to further researching my old home and to David's future book, "Ghosts of the Bluegrass." Perhaps we'll all have another story to tell.

Jill Richardson
Bloomfield, October 31, 2008

ACKNOWLEDGEMENTS

I would like to thank everyone who helped make this book a reality. For their expertise and knowledge, I am particularly grateful to parapsychological aficionados such as my good friend Kelly Atkins of Louisville; Starr and Jessi Chaney of PsyTech-Kentucky Ghost Hunters in Nicholasville; Nancy Walker; Willie "Windwalker" Gibson and his wife, Shmon; Cheryl Glassner; Patti and Bobby Zoeller; Suzy Johnson of the Garrs Lane Project; and Charla Stone of Utopia Dream Productions.

I would also like to thank friends and colleagues Barbara E. Cohen and Jerry Lee Rodgers – excellent writers in their own right – for their dedication, input and overall generosity as I worked on this project. Thank you to Mary Jo Harrod and David Williams as well, both wonderful writers who have been a tremendous help in proofing previous manuscripts, and to my good friend Jill "Hoof" Richardson for all her help and encouragement with this and other projects. John Schuler, thank you again for helping me a great deal with the complicated title searches that opened the doors to the past of so many of these old homes.

To Michelle Stone, my editor, Paula Cunningham and all the others at McClanahan Publishing House, Inc., thanks once again for your continued interest and support. I appreciate the assistance of James Asher for all the graphics in my books, and to Troy Harvey, who proved invaluable in helping me design my Web site *ghostsofoldlouisville.com*.

For their encouraging words, advice and/or assistance during this and previous projects, I'd like to recognize Lillie Trimble, Silvia, Miguel and Isabel Zañartú, Barbara Eilert, Michael Jackman, Sena Jeter Naslund, Charles Whaley, John Pfeiffer, Gregg Swem, Mark van Fleet,

Candyce Clifft, Cara Sabin, Kathi Lincoln, John Ashton, Jamie Roush, Gabriele Bosely, John and Tracey Fisher, Gwen Snow, Anetria Brownlee, Byron Summers, Barry Royalty, Sheila Berman, Jeff Maccoux, Viki Pidgeon, Catherine Seiberling Pond, Jamie Estes, Kat Gallagher, Karen Angelucci, Jane and Charlie Newsom, Bill and Joan Bosch, Uncle Leon, Don and Chris Lowe, Mama Skippy, and my brother and sister-in-law Travis and Marcie Domine.

I am also indebted to the many people who assisted me in conducting the research for this project, including the staffs of The Filson Historical Society, the Louisville Free Public Library, the Old Louisville Information Center, the Friends of Central Park, the library and archives at the University of Louisville, the Spalding University Library, the Conrad-Caldwell House, the Brennan House, the Louisville Ghost Hunters Society, the Dr. Thomas D. Clark History Center, the Louisville Landmarks Commission, Franklin & Hance, PSC and the Visitors Center in Historic Old Louisville. I'd especially like to acknowledge the assistance of Debra Richards, Judy Miller, Brian Pollock, Robin Wallace, Marion Wilson, Tom Owen, Deborah Stewart, Darnell Farris, Bob Keesar, Edward C. Halperin and Carolyn Brooks for their research; and I would be remiss to ignore the huge debt I owe previous writers and historians who have done so much to record the history of Old Louisville and the region. These include: Samuel W. Thomas, William Morgan, Wade Hall, George Yater, Tom Owen, Dr. Clyde Crews, Lynn Renault, and Melville O. Briney. Books such as Joanne Wheeler's *Louisville Landmarks*, the Louisville Guide by Luhan, Domer & Mahoney and John Kleber's *Encyclopedia of Louisville* proved invaluable in verifying and corroborating many of the historical and architectural details associated with my stories. A special word of thanks to the *Courier-Journal*, *The New York Times*, the *Atlanta Constitution* and the other newspapers around the country that have allowed me to cite and quote articles freely from their extensive archives.

Storytellers Roberta Simpson Brown and Dr. Lynwood Montell have been especially inspiring with their many entertaining tales of spooks and specters in this part of the country, and I've gained much useful information and valuable insight from Keven McQueen's well-written books about colorful Kentucky characters, Robert "Ghost

Walker" Parker's book about *Haunted Louisville,* and Thomas Freese's entertaining accounts of Shaker hauntings. Rose Pressey's book *My Haunted Family* and Robert Nunnely's *Mysterious Kentucky* have inspired me as well. I've also enjoyed reading Barry Royalty's articles about ghosts and hauntings in this area. Above all, I need to mention Hanz Holzer, the original ghost hunter, whose many fascinating books about the paranormal enthralled me in my younger years.

Thanks once again to the many individuals and neighborhood organizations in Old Louisville for all they do for the preservation and promotion of America's largest Victorian neighborhood. For their support and dedication to the neighborhood, I would like to make extra special mention of Michael Breeding; Carol and Mike McLaughlin; Peggy Cummins; Doug and Madonna Wilson; Gary and Diane Kleier; Rob and Maggie Young; Judy and Larry Franklin; Joan Stewart; Rhonda and Michael Williams; Barb Cullen; Jon Huffman; Susan Coleman; Scott and Sharon Risinger; Miss Wanda Stanley; Anne and Alan Bird; Don Driskell; John Reliford; Ed Turley; John Paul; Deb Riall; Mary Anne and the staff at the lovely Conrad-Caldwell House; Barb Donnelly; Ken Herndon, the Rosenbergs, Chuck and Sheelah Anderson; Linda Ewen of the Old Louisville Information Center; and Jane and Ron Harris of the Old Louisville Candy Company, makers of Happy Balls!, the official candy of Old Louisville. Also, a big thanks to the members of the Old Louisville Chamber of Commerce and to Mari Lively, Earlene Zimlich Bisig, Rick Tabb and Kevin Kouba of the Visitors Center in Old Louisville for all their hard work in promoting the neighborhood.

I need to thank all the residents and friends of Old Louisville who have opened their homes and shared their wonderful stories with me as well: the Carweils, David McNease and Larry Askins, Susan Shearer, Linda Gregory, Frances Mengel, the late Polly Clark, Mike and Judy Seale, Michelle Dutcher, Norma Ritz Williams, Kevin Milburn, Joan and Arnold Calentano, Doug Keller, Karen Keller, Herb and Gayle Warren, Kent Thompson, Jeff Perry, Dale Strange and Bill Gilbert, Lucie Blodgett, Mary Ann Culbertson, Robin Garland, Mitzi Long, Phoebe Netherton, Jill Montgomery, Susan Langford, Barb Donnelly, Rosemary Johnson and Greg Martin and his family.

In addition, a special debt of gratitude is owed to Doris Simms, Jim Wood, Susan Dallas, Lou Drescher, Nicole Twigg, Cinnamon Jawor and the many others at the Greater Louisville Convention and Visitors Bureau for their assistance in promoting the ghostly past of America's most haunted neighborhood.

Finally, thanks and cheers again to the colorful characters who have attended and/or still attend the weekly meals of the Thursday Night Dinner Club, which has since been renamed the Tuesday Night Dinner Club for obvious reasons. I look forward to many more nights and many more stories together.